Baddiley Church

THE OLD PARISH CHURCHES

OF CHESHIRE

Mike Salter

FOLLY PUBLICATIONS

ACKNOWLEDGEMENTS

The photographs and measured drawings in this book are mostly the product of the author's own fieldwork between 1977 and 1995. The old postcards reproduced in the book are from the author's collection. Thanks are due to Max Barfield who provided word processor facilities, checked the text, and did some of the driving for field trips in the 1990s. She also made available to the author a second camera and herself took the photograph of the jester headstop at Macclesfield on the back of the cover plus those of the pulpit, font, and tower at Mellor, the porch at Macclesfield, the lion's head mask at Nantwich, and tombs at Bunbury, Nantwich and Wilmslow.

ABOUT THIS BOOK

As with the other books about churches in this series (see the full list on the inside of the back cover) this book concentrates on the period prior to the Industrial Revolution of the late 18th century. Most furnishings and monuments after 1760 are not mentioned, although additions and alterations to the fabric usually are, although in less detail. New churches of after 1760 are not mentioned in the gazetteer, nor do they appear on the map. They are, however, listed towards the back of the book.

This book is intentionally very much a catalogue of dates and names, etc. It is intended as a field guide and for reference rather than to be read from cover to cover. Occasionally there is a comment about the setting of a church but on the whole little is said about their position or atmosphere. The amount of material given for a particular church in this book is not necessarily a true indication of how interesting or attractive the building may be. Some interesting and attractive features of the churches and their graveyards may lie outside the scope of this book. Visit them and judge for yourself. The gazetteer features Ordnance Survey grid references (these are the two letters and six digits which appears after each place-names and dedication) and the book is intended to be used in conjunction with 1:50,000 scale maps.

Plans redrawn from originals in the author's field notebooks are reproduced to a common scale of 1:400 (except that of St John at Chester at 1:600). The buildings were measured in metres and only metric scales are given. A system of hatching common to all the plans is used to denote the different periods of work. The plans should be treated with care and cross-referenced with the text, as there are some things that are difficult to convey on a small scale plan such as dressed stones of one period being reset or reused in a later period.

ABOUT THE AUTHOR

Mike Salter is 41 and has been a professional writer and publisher since he went on the Government Enterprise Allowance Scheme for unemployed people in 1988. He is particularly interested in the planning and layout of medieval buildings and has a huge collection of plans of churches and castles he has measured during tours (mostly by bicycle and motorcycle) of England, Ireland, Scotland and Wales since 1968. Wolverhampton born and bred, Mike now lives in an old cottage beside the Malvern Hills. His other interests include walking, model railways, board games, morris dancing, folk music, and playing percussion intruments.

ISBN 1 871731 23 2

Bidston Church

CONTENTS

Inside the front cover is a map of churches in the gazetteer.

INTRODUCTION

Cheshire was once a heavily forested border area on the boundary between England and Wales. Considerable parts of it were not cleared and settled until well into the medieval period. The area was converted to Christianity from Lindisfarne c653, and in 669 Osward, Bishop of York, was transferred to Lichfield. A legacy of this northern influence are many dedications among Cheshire churches to Northumbrian saints, with five each to St Chad and St Oswald and four to St Wilfrid. St Mary, however, is by far the most popular in Cheshire, however, with 26 dedications, whilst there are a dozen to St Peter, ten to St Michael, and nine to All Saints.

The Saxon period has left no certain standing fragments of buildings in Cheshire, although there are a pair of 9th century crosses at Sandbach, and 10th or 11th century crosses (all fragmentary) at Astbury, Bromborough, Cleulow, Macclesfield and Prestbury, whilst there are loose or reset carved stones of that period in half a dozen churches. The Norman invasion of 1066 had no immediate effect on Cheshire architecturally speaking. The Normans initially concentrated on building castles mostly of earth and wood and then turned to building cathedrals and abbeys. At Chester, a former Roman town, two churches which existed in the Saxon period were refounded as an abbey and cathedral respectively. The cathedral served only as such from 1075-95, when the Bishops transferred to Coventry, and the present church of St John, has no work earlier than c1130. Of that period are the crossing arches and a spacious aisled nave with arcades of round arches on huge round columns. The abbey (now, since 1540, the cathedral of a separate diocese of Chester) has earlier work, as its north transept is of c1100. The choir and NW tower there are also partly Norman, but later.

Sandbach Saxon Crosses

Norman doorway at Shocklach

The nave of St John's at Chester

Not until the mid 12th century did the Normans get round to rebuilding the stock of some twenty or so already existing Saxon churches in Cheshire, or erecting any new churches to serve freshly created parishes. Thirteen churches (Barthomley, Bowdon, Great Budworth, Davenham, Farndon, Frodsham, High Legh, Lymm, Northenden, Sandbach, Thornton-le-Moors, Weaverham and Wybunbury) are specifically mentioned in the Cheshire part of Domesday Book of 1086, and parish priests are mentioned in several other places. By 1140 there seem to have been about forty parish churches in Cheshire, and by 1200 this number had doubled. Commonly churches were built by lords close to their castles and manor houses and some still stand apart from the villages they serve. Until the wave of 19th century rebuilding at least thirty churches retained relics of the Norman period either in the form of fragments of the structure or a font.

Most Norman parish churches took the form of a nave in which the congregation stood, and a smaller chamber at the east end called a chancel in which the altar was placed. Usually there would be doorways towards the west end of the south and north walls of the nave, and sometimes there was another doorway specifically for use by the priest in the chancel south wall. The buildings were dimly lighted by windows of modest size with round arched heads set in embrasures which were splayed or opened out towards the interior. The walls would be plastered and painted with frescoes of Biblical scenes. In Cheshire remains of buildings of this kind are not as common and less complete than in neighbouring Shropshire. A hint of their appearance is given by the chapel at Prestbury, now entirely 18th century except an ornate west doorway (the building originally had an apse instead of a proper chancel), and by the somewhat altered nave and chancel at Bruera. Shocklach retains a Norman nave, and there are doorways at Barthomley, Church Lawton, and Shotwick. Of more ambitious buildings with aisled naves there are arcades at Bebington, Frodsham and Middlewich. Bebington may also have had a crossing tower, whilst Neston perhaps had a west tower. Norman fonts also survive in a few places, that at Mellor with bold but crude carvings of c1100 being the most notable.

Work of the 13th century is sparse in Cheshire parish churches, although something of the period survives in fifteen of them. St John's at Chester has a triforium arcade in the Transitional style of c1200 over the main nave arcades in which the pointed arch is used, yet the capitals still look Norman. The clerestory above it is still later and in the fully fledged Early English style. Windows began to be given pointed heads c1200 and then in the latter part of the century were made of two or three lights. Examples are rare in Cheshire, but Prestbury has a three light window in the chancel north wall, plus a set of arcades indicating a building of some size. A pair of arcades plus three arches supporting a tower remain at Acton.

Nantwich is an important instance of a big cruciform church with an aisled nave under construction for much of the 14th century. It was built by a lodge of masons assembled for the royal abbey of Vale Royal, who also worked at Backford, Handley, and Shotwick. The chancel lierne vault at Nantwich is a rarity in a parish church, and the octagonal upper part of the central tower is an uncommon feature too. Much of Thornton-le-Moors and Woodchurch are also 14th century, but both the scale and the details are more modest. Several large churches such as Astbury, Bunbury, Malpas, and Wilmslow retain a plan form and some details of the 14th century although as a result of remodelling they now outwardly appear to be of the end of the medieval period. There are not many examples in Cheshire of the typically Decorated flower-like window tracery patterns (Astbury has some modest examples) but reticulated or net-like tracery using the ogival arch introduced c1310 is common enough, as in the tower at Malpas. The tower at Eastham may be as early as c1300-10. It has diagonal buttresses (then a new innovation) and a broach spire.

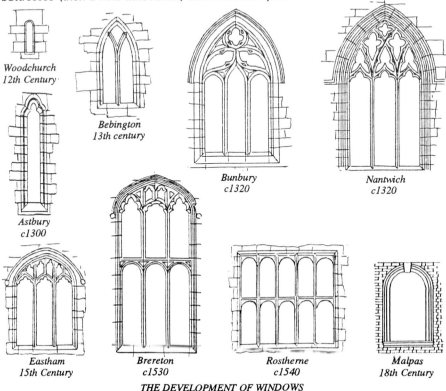

Woodchurch
12th Century

Bebington
13th century

Astbury
c1300

Bunbury
c1320

Nantwich
c1320

Eastham
15th Century

Brereton
c1530

Rostherne
c1540

Malpas
18th Century

THE DEVELOPMENT OF WINDOWS

The heavily restored timber-framed church at Lower Peover

Cheshire is celebrated for its timber framed churches. Most of these were aisled buildings with octagonal arcade piers such as Marton and Lower Peover which go back to the late 13th or 14th centuries and are the oldest of their type in Europe. Marton has an aisled tower similar to those of a small group of Essex churches. Baddiley, Chadkirk, High Legh, Holmes Chapel, Siddington, Swettenham, Warburton, Waverton, and Whitegate are also partly timber framed or retain wooden arcade piers, and other timber-framed churches are known to have existed prior to later rebuilding at Bosley, Church Minshull, Congleton, and Goostrey.

Towards the end of the 14th century the fashion changed from the florid Decorated style in vogue since c1300 to the new Perpendicular style with its emphasis on verticals. Panels rather than floral patterns now dominate window tracery. Early examples of the style in Cheshire are the chancel east windows of c1400 at Audlem and Nantwich. Not much work was executed between 1400 and 1470 but most churches in Cheshire were remodelled during the period 1470 to 1540, a boom period for ecclesiastical building in the county. Trade was flourishing, and Cheshire was then doing well out of excavating salt. Some buildings of this period are completely new foundations, Disley for instance having grown from what was originally a chantry chapel founded c1520. Long fully aisled buildings such as Mottram-in-Longendale are a characteristic of this period. Buildings of this type sometimes have no division between the nave and chancel as at Over, Weaverham and Northwich. The last has an polygonal east apse, an uncommon feature probably inspired by those at Lichfield Cathedral and St Michael's at Coventry. Astbury also has no division between nave and chancel, although there the layout has remained unchanged since the early 14th century. Late medieval additions at Astbury include a two storey south porch and a three storey west porch. Another tower-like porch is attached to the large Savage chapel at Macclesfield. Brereton is another instance of the nave and chancel being undivided. There the aisles flank the tower but not the chancel. Plempstall has an undivided nave and chancel with a north aisle only. A tower was only provided much later. Gawsworth is an interesting instance of what is thought to have originally been a modest nave with a south aisle and small chancel being remodelled a generation later as a wide unaisled single body with a west tower. At Brereton, Cheadle, Pott Shrigley, Marbury, and Wrenbury there are naves with north and south aisles and west towers mostly or entirely of this period.

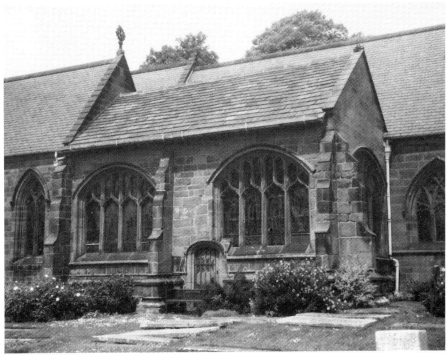

South chapel at Tarporley

Sixteen churches in Cheshire have a pair of late medieval arcades and another seven have just one arcade of this period. The arcades usually employ the four-centred arch characteristic of the Perpendicular style. Normally there are two orders with chamfered edges. Octagonal piers are common (occasionally with concave sides as at Over), and the type with four shafts and four diagonal hollows common in other counties in the 15th century occurs in Cheshire at Brerton, Bunbury, and Northwich. At Malpas the piers have eight lobes with hollows between them, at Barthomley they are chamfered-cornered squares with a shaft in the middle of each side, and at Great Budworth the piers have four sets of triple shafts with four hollows. At Astbury there are straight faces between four groups of triple shafts. Audlem has rare hexagonal piers. Capitals are usually moulded, but can be quite crude by the mid 16th century. Decorative motifs on them such as foliage, fleurons, shields or creatures are rare.

Many churches have late 15th or early 16th century clerestories often with a pattern of two windows of three or four lights to each bay. Only the east windows of chancels and their flanking chapels and the west windows of towers tend to have complex tracery. Windows in clerestories and aisle side walls are simpler, often having no tracery other than cusps in the heads of lights. Cusping is less common after 1500 and finally disappears by the mid 16th century. Battlements with or without pinnacles above the clerestory, chancel, and aisle walls are common.

Late medieval roofs of very low pitch with panels and bosses survive at Astbury, Barthomley, Cheadle, Chester St Mary's, Disley, Great Budworth, Malpas, and Northwich. Many other roofs of lesser distinction also remain. There are 17th century roofs of the hammer-beam type at Great Barrow, Handley, Hargrave, Harthill, Turvin, and another of as late as 1714 at Ashton-upon-Mersey.

Nearly all the medieval churches in Cheshire have towers. The 13th century tower at Acton is the earliest now surviving. Several 14th century towers were rebuilt later, but Astbury, Bebington and Eastham have good examples of that period with spires. The tower at Astbury is unusually positioned at the NW corner of the aisled nave. The majority of the towers (numbering 46 in all) are late 15th or 16th century and lie at the west end of the nave. Fine examples are at Barthomley, Great Budworth, Middlewich, Sandbach (rebuilt), Tarvin, Weaverham and Wybunbury. The bell openings in towers of this period are either of three lights or pairs of two lights. Often there are eight pinnacles and sometimes there are decorative motifs such as a frieze near the top or panelling on the battlements. At St Peter's at Chester, and Macclesfield (where the lowest stages of the towers served as porches), and also at Malpas, there are rib-vaults inside. Eighteen churches have late medieval porches, most of them positioned on the south side. Malpas has the best conventional porch. Astbury and Macclesfield have rare three storied porches looking like small towers.

Tower at Waverton

Tower at Nantwich

Tower at Barthomley

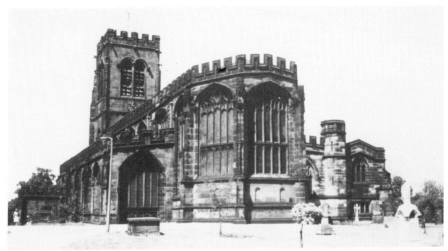

Northwich Church

Waverton Church

The period 1550 to 1700 is well represented by furnishings and monuments (see below) but structural remains are rarer. It seems funds for major building began to run out in the 1540s, schemes at Bebington and Tarvin being then left incomplete. The Elizabethan churches at Burleydam and Marple have gone, and nothing survives of extensive work of 1591 at Wybunbury or of the 17th century building at Wincle. Cheadle has a chancel of 1559 which is wider than the nave. A manorial chapel of brick was built at High Legh in 1581, and there are modest 17th century buildings at Harthill, Hargrave, and Lower Whitley, the last being of brick. These have mullioned windows with arched lights, as does the Legh Chapel at Macclesfield rebuilt in 1620. There is a building in this style as late as 1714 at Ashton-upon-Mersey. Lower Peover has a north chapel of c1650 in the Classical style. Several churches were damaged during the Civil War and it was for this reason that much of that at Farndon was rebuilt in 1658. Of the late 17th century are the chancels at Aston-by-Sutton and Great Barrow, the old church at Tushingham, and a manorial chapel at Tabley. Aston-by-Sutton was given a new nave to match in 1736.

The Jenkin Chapel at Saltersford is a small and modest stone building of 1733, much of Burton was rebuilt with ashlar in 1721, Frodsham has a pair of porches of that period, and there are several records of medieval stone spires being rebuilt during the 18th century. However, much 18th century work in Cheshire churches has brick used for the main walls and sometimes for the details as well. Examples are Congleton and Knutsford of the 1740s with Tuscan columns dividing off aisles which contain galleries, thus requiring an upper tier of windows, the brick shell around a medieval timber framed church at Holmes Chapel, the more modest buildings at Carrington and Somerford, and the churches of Burleydam and Macclesfield St Peter's. The last of these takes us into the period of the Industrial Revolution, the growth of suburbs, and the consequent building of many new churches in the 19th century and out of the era (from the earliest times to about 1760) covered by this book. In Cheshire there are nearly two hundred parish churches of the period 1760-to date, thus outnumbering the hundred or so older buildings. Many of the older churches were neglected during the late 17th and 18th centuries and by the 19th century they required substantial repair, and in a few instances enlargement to cope with increased congregations. In some cases there was an almost complete rebuilding, leaving little more than perhaps a roof, or a tower or chapel, some reset or reconstructed openings, arches and walls, and perhaps the odd defaced furnishing or monument from the medieval church. Sometimes old fonts and other furnishings were removed, left lying around outside or in pieces inside, until eventually a later generation reckoned them to be of interest and reinstated them.

Church of St John the Baptist at Knutsford

Pulpit at Mellor

Screen at Bunbury

By the time of the Reformation of the 1530s the interiors of churches that had originally been bare and poorly lighted in the 12th and 13th centuries had been transformed. Large new windows admitted more light despite being often filled with stained glass. Several churches have 15th, 16th, and 17th century glass although it is mostly just just a single surviving figure or shield from a larger design and quite a bit of it has been imported from continental churches in the 18th and 19th centuries, as at Birtles and Disley. Farndon has notable glass of c1660 depicting Cheshire Royalists in the Civil War. Floors were no longer of earth covered with rushes but were usually paved with slabs or tiles. Benches were provided for the congregation, most of the surviving examples having poppy-heads on the ends. Choir stalls, occasionally with hinged seats called miserichords, also remain in some of the bigger churches such at Nantwich. The growth of choirs was one reason why chancels had become larger, originally having been no more than mere small altar chambers in ordinary parish churches. Usually a chancel had on the south side two or three stone seats called sedilia for the use of the clergy. Near the sedilia would be a piscina or basin for rinsing out and draining the vessels used during masses. Sermons had become fashionable so pulpits began to be installed. The small pulpit carved from a single trunk at Mellor may be as early as c1330. Marbury has a later medieval wooden pulpit and Nantwich a stone one. Seventeenth century pulpits with tiers of blank arches on pilasters are common, and there are three decker 18th century pulpits at Baddiley, Plemstall, Shotwick and Tushingham.

In the later medieval period it was normal for chancels and chapels to be divided off by screens. A chapel screen of 1527 at Bunbury displays some of the earliest signs of the Renaissance having an effect on art and architecture in Cheshire. The chancel screen was often surmounted by a loft reached by a staircase in a side wall. The loft had a parapet facing the nave upon which was mounted a rood or crucifix and was used by musicians, important in an age when few churches could afford an organ. The lofts were also used by the performers of religious plays which had an important part in conveying Biblical stories and other ideas to a congregation mostly composed of people who could neither read nor write or understand Latin, the language in which services were conducted until the 16th century. No lofts remain in Cheshire but there are fine chancel screens remain at Astbury, Mobberley, and Siddington. At the Reformation the image of the rood and other "Popish" images of saints, etc, on screens, tombs, and in stained glass windows would be removed. Chancel screens were often cut down, and others were removed or restored almost out of existence in the 19th century. However they were not entirely out of fashion for there are 17th century examples at Middlewich and Prestbury.

Woodwork and stonework inside was painted and gilded to produce a riot of colour. Only faded fragments now remain of medieval mural paintings. After the Reformation many of them were painted over. In the 17th century texts such as The Commandments and psalms either painted on the walls or on boards became popular, Baddiley having boards of the 1660s with The Commandments, The Creed, and the Lord's Prayer. Old chests used to secure church plate are common, one at Lower Peover being carved from a single trunk. Later medieval octagonal fonts with blank panels or simple motifs on each side and 18th century baluster fonts are quite common, and there are a few dated fonts of the Restoration period of the 1660s. Communion rails are frequently late 17th century although older examples also survive. Several churches have 18th century brass chandeliers in the nave.

Font at Church Minshull

Font at Mellor

15th century tomb at Wilmslow

Brass, Chester

The stone knight at Rostherne is the earliest of the pre-Reformation effigies. Of alabaster are the knights of c1380-1400 at Acton, Bunbury, and Barthomley, the 15th century knights at Over Peover (two), Cheadle, and Macclesfield (four). Macclesfield has a fine collection of monuments, having also three of c1500-30, and others of later date. There is also another 16th century knight at Malpas, whilst Wilmslow has two tombs of c1540. Effigies engraved on flat cut-out brass sheets are not as common in Cheshire as in the more easterly and southerly English counties. Of c1460 are civilians at Chester St Peter's and Wilmslow, and there are 16th century civilians of at Macclesfield and Wybunbury. There is a knight of 1543 at Over. There are incised slabs with the engraved lines filled with black pitch at Great Budworth, Malpas, Over Peover (two), and Prestbury (four). That at Malpas and two of those at Prestbury are late 15th century, the rest are mid to late 16th century. A form of monument favoured especially for priests in the medieval period was a simple stone coffin with a floriated cross carved on the lid, as at Burton.

The tomb of Sir Hugh Calverley, d1394, at Bunbury

Tomb from Wybunbury now at Nantwich

There is a dearth of late 16th century three dimensional effigies but the 17th century has more to offer, with fine examples at Brereton, Bowdon, Chester St Mary's, Gawsworth (two), Macclesfield, and Malpas. Figures now sometimes lie on their side (Chester St Mary's) and kneeling children are common. One of the Gawsworth tombs has the deceased shown additionally underneath as a skeleton, and the same motif appears on a painted tablet of the 1620s at Over Peover, and in the 1690s with the skeleton upright at Chester St John's. The effigies of c1650-60 at Acton and Over Peover are the earliest in Cheshire to use white marble instead of alabaster. There are effigies of c1700 at Macclesfield and Mottram-in-Longendale but effigies of the deceased gradually came to be less fashionable. Many late 17th century monuments, and most of those of the 18th century, take the form of cartouches or tablets with long inscriptions normally ornamented with heraldry, cherubs, architectural surrounds, or symbols referring to the status or trade of the deceased. Examples are at Barthomley and Bruera. Peculiar to Cheshire are the series of 57 painted heraldic tablets painted by four generations of same family all named Randle Holme. Collections of them dating from 1611 to the early 18th century can be seen at Audlem, Backford, Bunbury, Stoak, and Thornton-le-Moors.

FURTHER READING

Cheshire Churches, John Leonard, Sigma, Wilmslow, 1990.
Cheshire Churches, Roland W. Morant, Countywise, Rockferry, 1989.
Cheshire, Nikolaus Pevsner & Edward Hubbard, 1971, Buildings of England series.
Old Cheshire Churches, Raymond Richards, Batsford, London, 1947.
There are thirteen well-illustrated articles about Cheshire churches and their contents by Fred Crossley published during and between the two world wars in the Journal of the Chester & North Wales Architectural, Archaeological & Historical Society, the Transactions of the Lancashire and Cheshire Antiquarian Society, and the Transactions of the Historic Society of Lancashire and Cheshire.

GAZETTEER OF CHESHIRE CHURCHES

ACTON   *St Mary*   SJ 632531

The oldest parts are the 13th century piers of the arcades and the three arches (later heightened) under the tower, which has lancets and pilasters. The tower top was rebuilt soon after it collapsed in 1757, having been weakened by a bombardment during the Civil War. The arcade capitals and much else date from a restoration by Austin and Paley in 1897-8, whilst the clerestory is of 1879. The north aisle is 14th century and has windows with cusped intersecting tracery. In the 15th century a new chancel was provided and the south aisle widened east of the tower. The chancel parapet is 17th century and there is a 19th century vestry. Of the 12th century are the font with arches and alternating flowers and figures, and the several loose stones in the south aisle carved with intersecting arches and figures. One shows Christ with angels on either side. Ancient furnishings include the dado of a Jacobean screen, a screen of 1685, a communion rail, and an 18th century brass chandelier. A tomb recess with a panelled back in the north aisle contains an alabaster effigy of Sir William Mainwaring, d1399. There are white recumbent effigies of Sir Richard Wilbraham, d1643 and his wife, and there are tablets to a lady of the Wilbraham family, d1632, and Samuel Edgley, d1721.

Acton Church

Ashton-Upon-Mersey Church

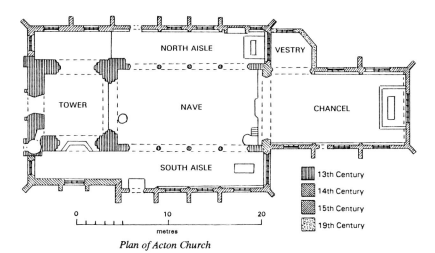

Plan of Acton Church

13th Century
14th Century
15th Century
19th Century

ASHTON-UPON-MERSEY   *St Martin*   SJ 773930

The 17th century-looking mullioned windows with arched lights are actually of a rebuilding of 1714. The double-hammerbeam roof is probably also of that period, and possibly also the east and west windows with intersecting tracery, if they are not Victorian. Box pews have been used to provide material for panelling the chancel. There is an 18th century baluster font. The SE tower with a half-timbered top is an addition of 1887. There are old stocks in a recess in the churchyard wall.

Astbury Church from the south

ASTBURY   *St Mary*   SJ 846615

The church has an unusual layout. The main body and aisles are both very wide, although the width of the main body decreases towards the east. There are seven bays with only a splendid (but partly rebuilt) screen of c1500 dividing the nave from the chancel. The arcades and the low-pitched roofs with camber-beams and many bosses are 15th century and so is the whole of the west end with a thin three-storey porch which was intended to have a vaulted ceiling. Light pours into the nave through a clerestory of four-light windows and the double-transomed four light windows on either the side of the porch. The north and south porches, the latter a two storey structure, are also 15th century. The north chapel has late 13th century windows with Y-tracery, and there are similar windows but with cusps (i.e. of c1300-10) in the north and south aisles. Of the same period are the south doorway, and the west responds of the arcades. The tower projecting north beyond the north aisle has a recessed spire and is mid to late 14th century.

The church contains much of interest. There is a second screen of c1500 closing off one of the chapels. The pulpit with two tiers of blank arches is Jacobean. The font cover and the wooden eagle lectern may be of the same period or slightly later. The communion rail is certainly mid 17th century. The south door with fleurons is 15th century. The clerestory has on the north side a short section of wall painting of c1500 showing a coat of arms and what is probably the Virgin blessing St George. From the clerestory are fragments of glass of c1500 now in the north aisle west window. Other fragments remain in the south aisle west window and one south window. The east windows have Victorian glass. In the north aisle is part of an 11th century cross-shaft with interlace ornament. There is an effigy of a late 14th century knight in the south chapel. There are other worn 14th century effigies of a priest and a knight said to be Ralph Brereton. On the north side of the chancel is an effigy of Lady Egerton, d1609, and in the south chapel is a tomb chest with shields and initials of Thomas Bellot, with the date 1654.

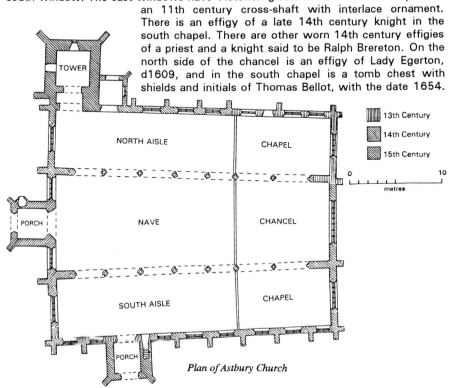

Plan of Astbury Church

Acton Church

ASTON-BY-SUTTON

St Peter   SJ 555785

Astbury Church from the west

In the 1520s Thomas and Bridget Aston built a new chapel (probably at least partly timber framed) on the site of a 12th century building. It was "much defaced" in the Civil War. The present chancel was built in 1697 for Sir Willoughby Aston, probably with Vanburgh as the architect. It has an east front with two niches, a circular window, and a pedimental gable. Within it is a tablet to Sir Thomas and John Aston, erected in 1697, another to Sir Willoughby, d1702, and his wife, d1712, and several others to members of the same family. The nave with arched windows with pilasters and an open bell-cupola on a projection from the west front is a Georgian addition of 1736. The church was badly damaged in November 1940 when a German bomb landed close alongside. In the restoration of 1951 the south porch was rebuilt but the former organ chamber (which was wrecked) was not replaced.

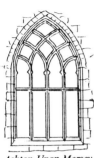

Ashton-Upon-Mersey

Aston-by-Sutton Church

Audlem Church

AUDLEM   *St James*   SJ 659437

The oldest feature is the late 13th century south doorway with one order of shafts. The priest's doorway, the lower part of the NW tower, the north aisle with its two-light windows, and the narrow south aisle masonry with traces of windows smaller and lower than the present ones between deep buttresses are early 14th century. At the end of the 14th century the church was remodelled and given new lofty arcades and an embattled clerestory of twelve closely set windows. The east window, reset in a lengthened east end of 1885-6 by Lynam and Rickman, and the fine roofs with few bosses are probably of the same period. The chancel is rather irregularly shaped. The pulpit with two tiers of blank arches is Jacobean and the panelled base and stem of the font are of about the same period. There is a 13th century chest. The brass chandelier was donated in 1751. The stained glass is all Victorian. There are four painted heraldic tablets dating from 1611 to 1708.

BACKFORD   *St Oswald*   SJ 398718

The long low chancel with an east window with intersecting tracery is early 14th century. The west tower with eight pinnacles and renewed gargoyles is 15th century but the arch to the nave may be 14th century. The nave is of 1877-9 by Ewan Christian, replacing a Classical style structure of 1728-31. There are several 17th century heraldic tablets. In the churchyard is a crude 18th century sundial.

BADDILEY   *St Michael*   SJ 605503

This is a timber framed church, although the nave was encased in brick in 1811. The tympanum dated 1663 has the Royal Arms, the Creed, the Lord's Prayer, and the Commandments. The communion rail is dated 1701 and there are box pews and a three decker pulpit. An early 16th century bench end has a poppy head and linenfold panelling. There is a monument to Sir Thomas Mainwaring, d1726.

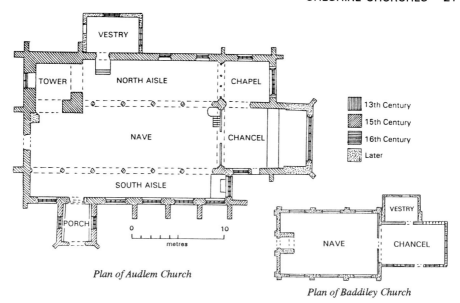

Plan of Audlem Church

13th Century
15th Century
16th Century
Later

Plan of Baddiley Church

Tympanum with the Royal Arms, Baddiley

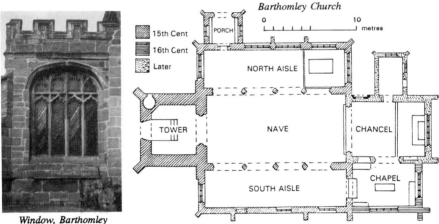

Window, Barthomley

Barthomley Church

15th Cent
16th Cent
Later

PORCH

NORTH AISLE

TOWER

NAVE

CHANCEL

SOUTH AISLE

CHAPEL

0   10
metres

Plan of Barthomley Church

BARTHOMLEY   *St Bertoline*   SJ 767524

The dedication is a very rare one. The church is mostly 15th century and has a west tower with eight pinnacles, and an embattled clerestory of eight close-set windows over arcades of four bays with piers which are chamfered squares with four attached shafts. The aisles are also embattled and there are fine contemporary roofs. A south doorway has been removed. The Crewe chapel of c1528 on the south side has windows with uncusped tracery and an original screen. It contains a late 14th century alabaster effigy of a knight, probably Sir Robert Foulshurst, an effigy of Rector Robert Foulshurst, d1529, and several monuments to the Crewe family, notably those of Anne, d1711, and John, d1749. The chancel, including the arch to the nave and the arcade to the chapel, is entirely of 1925-6 by Austin and Paley. Reset on the north side is a blocked Norman doorway with one order of columns with leaf capitals and an arch decorated with chevrons. There are five Baroque sculptured medallions of saints from France or Flanders. In 1643 Major Connaught attacked a force of Parliamentarians in the church. They took refuge in the tower but were smoked into submission and then stripped and several of them killed.

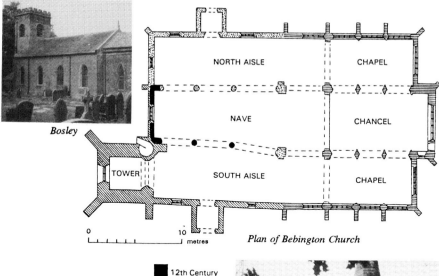

Bosley

Plan of Bebington Church

0 _____ 10
metres

■ 12th Century
▨ 14th Century
▤ 16th Century
▨ 19th Century

BEBINGTON   *St Andrew*   SJ 333839

The north aisle was added in 1846, material from the old north wall being reused. The north arcade is a replica of the eastern two bays of the south arcade, which are Norman and have scalloped capitals on round piers and single stepped arches. It appears that there was a Norman crossing too, presumably with a central tower. In c1300 the south aisle was rebuilt wider and longer, and a generation or two later the arcade was lengthened and a diagonally buttressed tower with broach-spire added west of the south aisle. The chancel with its flanking chapels and the transepts are 16th century, part of an incomplete scheme for rebuilding the whole church. The chapels have transomed windows in embrasures which continue down with panelling inside. The font is of uncertain date. Three of the stalls have misericords carved respectively with a bearded face, a pelican, and a dolphin. There are four traceried stall ends with poppy-heads.

Tower, Bebington

BIDSTON   *St Oswald*   SJ 283903

The shields over the west doorway date the west tower to 1504-21. The doorway has a four-centered head with a label moulding and has above it a window with an ogival hoodmould. The rest of the 13th century church was entirely rebuilt in 1855.

BIRTLES   *St Catherine*   SJ 863748

The building is of 1840 but contains 16th and 17th century glass from the Netherlands, a pulpit dated 1686, a medieval eagle lectern, and reused fragments of old woodwork, all brought in by Thomas Hibbert Birtles Hall.

BOSLEY   *St Mary*   SJ 918655

The small west tower is late medieval. The nave of 1777 and the chancel of 1834 are both of brick. The original nave and chancel were timber framed structures. Inside is a mid 17th century pulpit with detached angle colonettes.

BOWDON   *St Mary*   SJ 758868

The church, a large building with wide aisles and a big west tower, is entirely of the rebuilding of 1858-60 by W.H. Brakspear. However it retains its early 16th century roofs. Before the rebuilding the south aisle had a series of late 16th century square-headed four-light transomed windows and there were some reset Norman stones. In the north transept are fragments of a delicately carved medieval reredos, screen, or tomb, plus carved fragments of the Saxon and Norman periods and some small 14th century heads. What was once thought to be the defaced effigy of a medieval priest may be a 10th century figure of Christ. There are effigies of an early 14th century knight and of William Brereton, d1630, and his wife. The monuments of 1734 and 1735 to the 1st Earl of Warrington, and Langham and Henry Booth are both by Andrew Carpenter. The monument to Thomas Assheton Smith, d1774 is by Richard Westmacott.

0   3 m   CHANCEL

NAVE

VESTRY   TOWER

Brereton Church

Plan of Bosley Church

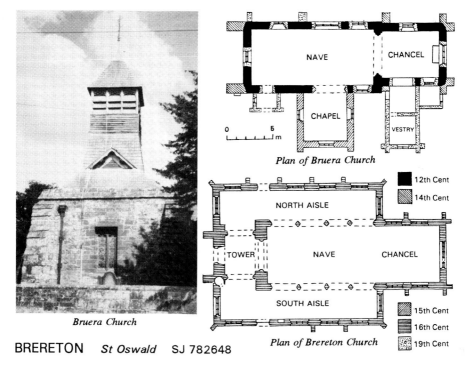

Plan of Bruera Church

NAVE CHANCEL

CHAPEL VESTRY

0 5 m

NORTH AISLE

TOWER NAVE CHANCEL

SOUTH AISLE

Bruera Church

Plan of Brereton Church

■ 12th Cent
▨ 14th Cent
▨ 15th Cent
▥ 16th Cent
▦ 19th Cent

BRERETON   *St Oswald*   SJ 782648

The church lies close to the Elizabethan hall and is entirely early 16th century. Until then the church here seems to have been a timber building ranking only as a chapel-of-ease to Astbury. It has an embattled chancel of two bays with the window lights simply arched below a transom but cusped and arched above, nave arcades of four bays, a west tower embraced by the west ends of the aisles, and low pitched panelled roofs. The font with simple geometric motifs is dated 1660. There are three-quarter frontal facing effigies of William Smethwick, d1643, and his wife, plus a monument to Sir William Brereton, d1618.

BROMBOROUGH   *St Barnabas*   SJ 349823

The church is a large building of 1862-4 by Sir George Gilbert Scott replacing a Norman building with two south doorways. Outside it are a damaged cross head and part of a shaft with interlace of a Saxon cross.

BRUERA   *St Mary*   SJ 437605

Much of the fabric is Norman, and of that period are the ornamented stones inside the south doorway and the south respond of the chancel arch with three shafts, upon one of which are four single beak-heads. The arch has two orders and a roll. The other respond, now renewed, was damaged by the pulpit being placed against it. The east window and several others plus the buttresses are 14th century and the chapel on the south side of the nave is 15th century. The shingled bell-turret with a spire is of the restoration of 1896 by W. M. Boden for the Duke of Westminster. The baluster font is probably late 17th century. There are monuments with putti to Sir Ellis Cunliffe, d1769, and Sir Robert Cunliffe, d1778, the latter by Nollekens.

BUNBURY   *St Boniface*   SJ 569581

The splendid 14th century chancel has flowing tracery in the east window (it once contained glass dated 1343), a fine doorway to an altered treasury on the north side, and ogival heads on the tomb recesses and the piscina and sedilia. Of the same period are the south porch, the lower parts of the west tower which is engaged by the aisles and has an arch with continuous mouldings towards the nave, and the west responds of the eight bay arcades. Sir Hugh Calveley, whose alabaster tomb chest and effigy lie in the middle of the chancel, had the church made collegiate in 1386 with a master, submaster, five chaplains, and two chaunters with two choristers. At the turn of the 15th and 16th centuries high new arcades were provided, the north aisle rebuilt from the ground, and the south aisle given new windows. The leaning north arcade has spandrels with angels. Battlements with pinnacles were then added to the aisle walls. The chancel east gable is oddly truncated, having fallen in the 1750s and never been restored to its original form. The high parapet of openwork panelling on the north aisle dates only from 1840 whilst the clerestory is of 1863-6 by Pennington and Bridgen. The south chapel was added by Sir Ralph Egerton, who is depicted kneeling on a small brass dated 1527. There are also two 13th century coffin lids with foliated crosses and effigies of an early 14th century knight and lady, a late 14th or early 15th century knight, a lady of c1375 (Joan de Spurstow), and a 14th or 15th century civilian, all of them rather defaced and not currently on show. There is an effigy in the chancel of the centenarian Sir George Beeston, d1601, and there is a painted tablet to George Spurstow, d1669. At the west end of the south aisle are loose fragments from a Norman doorway, and a standing effigy of Jane Johnson, d1741, banished by an incumbent c1760 and buried, but in the 19th century accidentally discovered and restored. The fragments painted with figures of saints from the 15th century parclose screens which once divided off chapels at the east end of each aisle were restored in 1988. The church was damaged during an attack upon it in 1643.

Bunbury Church

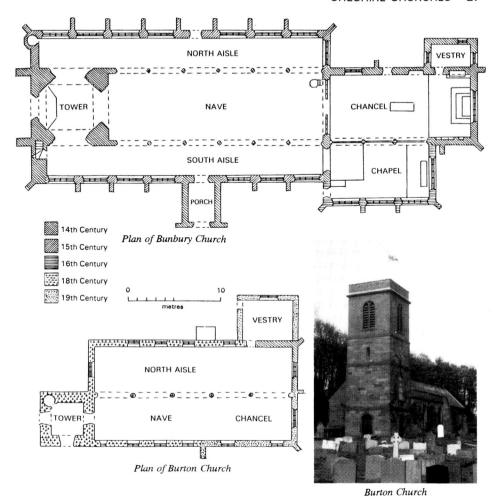

Plan of Bunbury Church

14th Century
15th Century
16th Century
18th Century
19th Century

0   metres   10

Plan of Burton Church

Burton Church

BURLEYDAM   *St Michael*   SJ 606426

This wide brick church with transepts, arched windows, and a three bay west front with a pediment was built in 1769 for the Cotton family of Combermere Abbey. The east end was extended in 1886.

BURTON   *St Nicholas*   SJ 317744

The church is twin naved with a coarse arcade of five bays and a tower with Y-traceried bell-openings. It is mostly of 1721, but the chancel was rebuilt in 1870 and the east end of the north chapel is a survival of c1300 with a window with intersecting tracery. In the porch are two large scalloped Norman capitals from an arcade removed during the rebuilding. There is a 13th century coffin lid with a foliated cross with long leaf trails. The 18th century communion rail has alternate balusters twisted.

BURWARDSLEY *St John* SJ 515565

An inscription suggests the church was remodelled in 1795 but the building looks 17th century, having mullioned windows with arched lights and a shaft with a capital in the west window. The chancel, and probably also the bell turret, are of 1884-9. The organ looks Late Georgian.

CARRINGTON *St George* SJ 728926

This brick building of four bays with arched windows is of 1757-9, but the chancel is of 1872. Original are the box pews, two family pews, and the altered pulpit.

CHADKIRK *St Chad* SJ 940903

Near the canal in Lower Chadkirk Lane is a chapel with a timber framed 16th century chancel. The south side and the font are of 1747. In that year the chapel returned to the Anglicans after being used by Puritans. Previous to that the Davenport family used it as a stable. Parts of the building are of the 1860s. It became redundant in 1971 and was restored by Stockport Borough Council in 1994.

CHEADLE *St Mary* SJ 856887

The church is entirely in the Late Perpendicular style. The aisles were completed c1528, and the nave with its clerestory and roof, the fine south porch, and the west tower are of the same period. The date 1634 on the porch refers to repairs. The chancel, much wider than the nave, was built in 1556-8 by Lady Catherine Buckley, former abbess of the nunnery of Godstow in Bedfordshire. The north chapel screen has the date 1529 and an inscription referring to Sir John Savage, whilst the south chapel screen bears the Brereton family rebus and has a dado with linenfold panelling (the chapels lie in the aisle east ends). The chancel screen has been mostly renewed. There are fragments of old glass in the south chapel windows. Two effigies of knights of c1470 now both on one tomb chest are probably of members of the Handford family. There is also an effigy of Sir Thomas Brereton, d1673.

17th Century
19th Century

Burwardsley: plan

0   5
⌊_⌊_⌊_⌊_⌊_⌊⌋ m

Cheadle Church

Chadkirk Chapel

Chancel at Cheadle

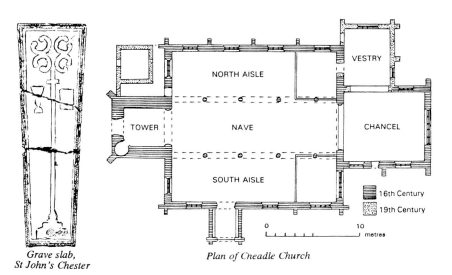

Grave slab,
St John's Chester

Plan of Cheadle Church

CHESTER *Holy Trinity* SJ 403663

This building of 1865-9 by James Harrison (completed after his death by Kelly and Edwards) now serves as the Guildhall. It contains an effigy of John Whitmore, d1374, now hidden under the floor, and a brass which is a palimpsest, the reverse showing part of an early 16th century knight. The original building, which in 1843 had a north aisle with a brick outer casing, was probably 14th century, although the east end and south side were rebuilt in 1680. The church once had a spire which needed much rebuilding in the 1770s and was taken down for safety in 1811.

Two views of the ruined east end, St John's Chester

CHESTER   *St John Baptist*   SJ 409661

The church existed in Saxon times and was made collegiate in 1057 by Leofric, Earl of Mercia. In 1075 Peter, Bishop of Lichfield transferred to Chester and St John's became a cathedral until his successor moved to Coventry in 1095. The oldest parts of the present building are probably of c1100-20, and represent a Norman crossing, now with the transepts shorn off, one bay of the original chancel, and several bays of an aisled nave with double stepped arches upon study round columns with scalloped capitals. The triforium stage in the nave with pointed arches is of the end of the 12th century and the clerestory is 13th century. Vaulting shafts rise from the triforium but no vaults survive (they were probably never built). The eastern part of the church, with a Norman arch to a former Lady Chapel, and 14th century arches to side-chapels, has been ruinous since the Dissolution, when the former abbey church was taken over as the cathedral of a new diocese of Chester and St John's was downgraded in importance. East of where the south transept would have been is a room of c1300 with a central pier called the Chapter House. The west front has an off-balance appearance with two towers of differing sizes. The larger NW tower, which is 16th century, has been ruined since the top fell and destroyed the original north porch in 1881. A new porch was built in 1882. Much of the exterior of the church dates from restorations by R.C.Hussey in 1859-66 and 1886-7. See p5.

The small square font with vegetable motifs is probably of c1660. In the SE chapel are parts of a reredos of 1692. A wall painting of St John the Baptist in the north aisle east respond is now barely visible. There are two brass chandeliers given in 1722. The monuments include effigies of an early 14th century cross-legged knight and a priest of the same period, plus a slab depicting the upper half of Agnes de Ridleigh, d1347 in relief. There are several 17th century painted tablets and a skeleton holds an inscription to Diana Warburton, d1693. There is a bust in relief in a medallion to Cecil Warburton, d1729.

CHESTER   *St Mary-on-the-hill*   SJ 406659

The church is Norman in origin (it served the nearby castle) but the exterior dates mostly from restorations of 1861-2 and 1890-1 by James Harrison and J.P.Seddon respectively. During the latter restoration the north porch was added. The tower base has a worn early 16th century doorway. The tower arch and chancel arch are 14th century and the three bay arcades with octagonal piers are late 15th century. The nave has a fine camber-beam roof with many bosses. The south aisle windows have reveals on animal corbels. The south chapel was built c1443 but collapsed in 1661. It belonged to the Earl of Shrewsbury and was rebuilt in 1693, when the chancel arch responds were renewed. On the south aisle east wall are slight traces of a wall painting with a Crucifixion and several other figures, one a king. The window in this wall includes old glass with a series of Passion shields and the Brereton rebus. There are effigies of Thomas Gamul, d1616, and his wife (who had the tomb erected), plus some of their children who died young. There is an effigy of Philip Oldfield, d1616, lying on his side, and in the north aisle are 17th century tablets to the Randle Holme family. Other monuments were destroyed when the Troubeck chapel on the south side collapsed in 1661, partly through neglect and partly through damage received during a bombardment during the siege of 1645.

CHAPEL

CHAPEL

CHAPEL

TOWER

NORTH AISLE

NAVE

SOUTH AISLE

■	12th Century
⫿	13th Century
◩	14th Century
◪	15th Century
▦	16th Century
▨	Later

TOWER

0   10
metres

1:600 scale plan of St John's, Chester

CHESTER   *St Michael*   SJ 406661

Much of the church is of 1849-50 by James Harrison, but there is a 15th century north arcade with fleurons on the capitals, and a chancel roof of 1496, now too narrow as a result of widening in 1678. Bridge Street Row passes below the tower. The church was declared redundant in 1972 and is now used as a Heritage Centre. In the 17th century it had a priest's room on columns over the west doorway.

CHESTER   *St Nicholas*   SJ 406664

On the south side is some medieval work, probably from the enlargement of 1488. In 1854-5 Harrison adapted the chapel as a concert hall and built a new front. It now serves as a supermarket.

CHESTER   *St Olave*   SJ 408660

This medieval chapel in Lower Bridge Street was mostly rebuilt in 1859.

CHESTER   *St Peter*   SJ 404664

The church is 14th century but with a 15th century outer north aisle. There has been much 17th, 18th, and 19th century rebuilding and restoration. In particular there were continual problems with a spire which after several rebuildings was taken down. The tower is embraced by the nave and aisle and has an inserted vault with a large hole for the bell-ropes. There is a brass showing a civilian of c1460.

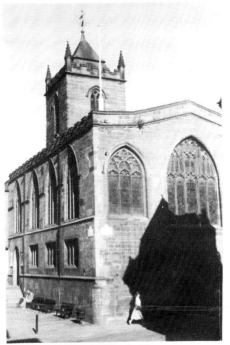

St Peter's Church, Chester

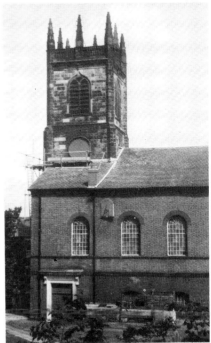

Congleton Church

CHRISTLETON   *St James*   SJ 441658

The tower is partly 15th century, but its top goes with the church which was built in 1875-7 by Butterfield and has his typical internal contrasting colours. The church was occupied by a Parliamentarian force during the siege of Chester in 1645, and was damaged when the garrison made a sally to attack it. Repairs were carried out in 1678 and a new brick church was built in 1738.

CHURCH LAWTON   *All Saints*   SJ 822558

The nave is a brick structure of 1803 with arched windows flanked by lunettes. The south doorway is Norman and has scalloped capitals and chevrons on the arch. The 16th century west tower bears a chalice and large initials of the rector John Byber, d1555. Similar initials appear on his plain tomb chest inside the church.

CHURCH MINSHULL   *St Bartholomew*   SJ 666606

The original timber framed church was given a west tower in 1702 and then was rebuilt in brick in 1704 at a cost of £2,500. The north doorway and round window over it have bolection mouldings typical of that period. The interior is divided into a nave and aisles of four bays by round piers with semi-circular arches, and there is a shallow apse. The south porch and the tracery in the arched windows must be of the restoration of 1861. The font is of 1717. A painted 17th century heraldic tablet survives from the earlier church. See page 13.

CONGLETON   *St Peter*   SJ 859628

Originally this was a 15th century timber framed building with aisles and a porch added in 1613, and a new chancel added in 1640, also timber framed. As rebuilt in 1740-2 the church is a brick building of seven bays with two tiers of windows and a Venetian east window and an angle-porch. Inside are a coved ceiling and three galleries with Tuscan columns, plus an original baluster font and a reredos. On either side of the east window are paintings of St Peter and St Paul, painted by Edward Penny in 1748. The tower is Gothick and was completed in 1786. The Jacobean font with detached angle-colonettes has come from Astbury.

CONGLETON   *St James*   SJ 854631

In the church built by James Trubshaw in 1847-8 for the Church Commissioners is an ornate mid 17th century Flemish pulpit.

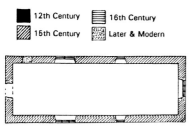

■ 12th Century   ▤ 16th Century
▨ 15th Century   ▦ Later & Modern

Plan of St Olave's Church, Chester

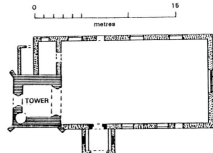

Plan of Church Lawton Church

Tower at Daresbury

Eastham Tower

DARESBURY   *All Saints*   SJ 581828

The church is best known for its Lewis Carroll stained glass window. It was rebuilt in 1870-2 by Paley and Austin (the nave was 13th century) except for the 15th century west tower. The pulpit with angle figure brackets is probably Jacobean.

DAVENHAM   *St Wilfred*   SJ 663713

This was once a 14th century building (on the site of a church mentioned in Domesday Book) with arcades of four bays and aisles which engaged the west tower, but it now has no ancient features. The chancel was rebuilt in 1680, 1795, and 1870, the nave was rebuilt in 1844, the tower and spire are of 1850, and transepts were added in 1870. The owners of Leftwich Hall had a small chapel on the north side. A new spire was built in 1680.

DISLEY   *St Mary*   SJ 974845

The west tower with a blocked arch and the fine roof with many bosses are all that survive of a chantry chapel built by Sir Piers Legh, d1527. It was not consecrated until 1558 when it became a parish church at the request of Sir Peter Legh. The rest of the building was rebuilt in 1824-35 and aisles were then added. The south porch was then rebuilt in front of the tower west doorway. The east window has glass dated 1535, signed Steynfrit, and evidently made in Holland or Switzerland. There are fragments of old glass in some of the other windows. There are monuments to George Barbor, d1779, and Richard Orford, 1791.

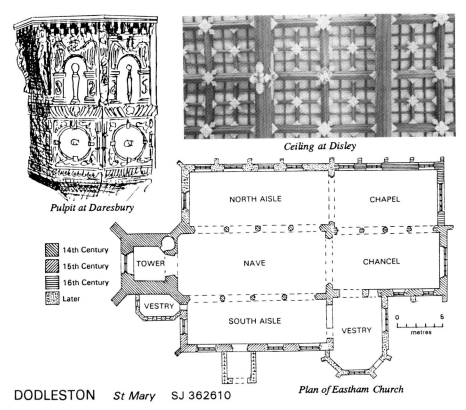

Ceiling at Disley

Pulpit at Daresbury

14th Century
15th Century
16th Century
Later

TOWER

VESTRY

NORTH AISLE

NAVE

SOUTH AISLE

CHAPEL

CHANCEL

VESTRY

0   5
metres

Plan of Eastham Church

DODLESTON   *St Mary*   SJ 362610

In 1870 Douglas rebuilt the whole of the medieval church (which had a 13th century chancel) except the lower part of the west tower. The font may be 17th century.

EASTHAM   *St Mary*   SJ 361800

Of the 14th century are the four bay arcades and the big west tower with diagonal buttresses on all four corners and a spire which was rebuilt in 1751. The north chapel is 16th century but the arcade between it and what was once a 13th century chancel and most of the exterior features of the church are of the restoration of the 1870s by David Walker. The south aisle was rebuilt in the 15th century. The font is probably 13th century. There are tomb chests of Sir William Stanley, d1612, and Sir Rowland Stanley, d1613.

ECCLESTON   *St Mary*   SJ 362610

The medieval church was entirely rebuilt in 1809 by Porden of Chester for Earl Grosvenor, and a chancel was added in 1853. This building was in turn replaced by a church of 1899 designed by G.F.Bodley for the 1st Duke of Westminster on a nearby site at a cost of £40,000.

EGERTON   SJ 515506

In a field near the hall are two featureless walls of a medieval domestic chapel.

FARNDON   *St Chad*   SJ 414544

Only the lower parts of the west tower are medieval. The church was badly damaged in the Civil War when it was used as a strongpoint. The round piers bearing single chamfered arches, the clerestory, and parts of the chancel are of the rebuilding of 1658. The aisle windows are probably of the restoration of 1869 by Kelly and Edwards. One window has 17th century glass depicting Cheshire Royalists in the time of the Civil War. There is a defaced effigy of a mid 14th century knight.

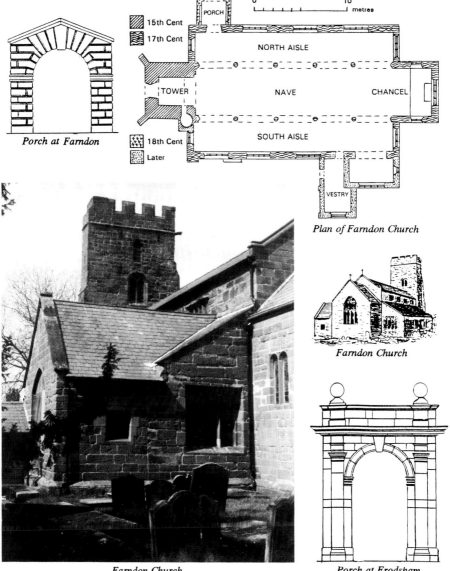

Porch at Farndon

15th Cent
17th Cent
18th Cent
Later

Plan of Farndon Church

Farndon Church

Farndon Church

Porch at Frodsham

Frodsham Church

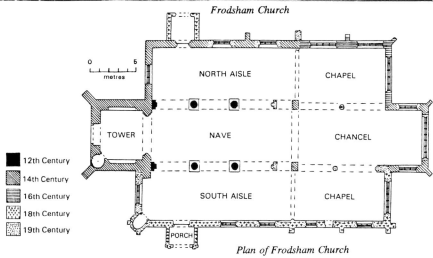

12th Century
14th Century
16th Century
18th Century
19th Century

O ____ 5
metres

NORTH AISLE

CHAPEL

TOWER

NAVE

CHANCEL

SOUTH AISLE

CHAPEL

PORCH

Plan of Frodsham Church

FRODSHAM *St Laurence* SJ 521773

Much of the church was rebuilt by Bodley and Garner in 1880-3. The western parts of the north arcade and clerestory are of c1170-85. The aisle itself is 14th century, as is the chancel, which was lengthened in the 15th century, with a fine seven light east window. The north chapel is early 16th century and contains a reredos of c1700. The west tower is late 14th or early 15th century and has high blocked arches on the north and south sides and contains reset sculptured stones of the Saxon and Norman periods with figures and chevrons respectively. The porches are of 1715 and 1724 respectively, the south aisle having been rebuilt at the latter date, and again in 1882. The communion rail with twisted balusters is of c1700.

GAWSWORTH   *St James*   SJ 890697

The church is delightfully situated by a pool in the estate. The wide nave is late 15th century and the south porch, west tower, and the chancel, undivided from the nave except by a screen of 1894, are of the time of Randle Flitton, rector from 1497 to 1536. The nave south side seems to be of two periods so perhaps there was originally a south aisle and nave corresponding in width to what is now just nave. The tower and nave are embattled with pinnacles. The font with two shields in panels on each of eight sides, and some fragments of old glass are also of c1500-30. In the chancel are tomb chests with effigies of Francis Fitton, d1608 (also depicted as a skeleton), Sir Edward Fitton, d1619, and his wife, Dame Alice Fitton, d1627, and Sir Edward Fitton, d1643.

GOOSTREY   *St Luke*   SJ 779700

A 15th century font with leaf quatrefoils and a panelled stem survives in the brick church of 1792-6 with a west tower, arched windows, and a rusticated south doorway. It cost £1,700. The old church was a timber framed. Its aisles were enlarged in 1668, and the Jodrells added a private north chapel c1712.

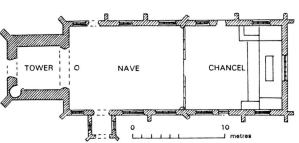

Plan of Gawsworth Church

Gawsworth Church   *Grappenhall Church*

GRAPPENHALL   *St Wilfred*   SJ 639864

A corbel table visible outside shows that the nave south wall is partly Norman, and the oblong font with blank arcading is also of that period. One of the Boydell family who founded a chantry here c1334 has his effigy in the chancel. He built the south chapel with its square-headed windows in the Decorated style containing fragments of contemporary glass. The west tower and the aisled nave of seven bays are of the years leading up to 1539, the date appearing on one of the octagonal arcade piers. A clerestory was added in 1833 but it must have been remodelled during the restoration of 1874 by Austin and Paley when the 14th century south aisle was rebuilt. Their work also includes the long north transept and the east window, the original east window having been transferred into the north aisle. The churchyard has a column sundial dated 1714 and old stocks.

GREAT BARROW   *St Bartholomew*   SJ 470684

Only the north arcade of depressed arches is likely to be medieval. A Dean of Chester Cathedral had the chancel rebuilt in 1671. It has mullioned windows and a hammerbeam truss decorated with shields. The font is dated 1713 and the west tower is of 1744 when there was considerable rebuilding after the steeple was described as ruinous, the nave walls as bulging out dangerously, and the roof much decayed. The nave exterior was restored by Douglas in 1883.

Great Budworth Church

Great Barrow Church

GREAT BUDWORTH

St Mary   SJ 665775

The church is a large, all-embattled building with a west tower, a nave and aisles of six bays, and a chancel with chapels. The reticulated east window and the long north transept are of c1330, but the rest is all of c1490-1530. Richard Starkey left money for building a rood loft in 1527. The tower is similar to that at Northwich, and was probably also designed by the mason Richard Hunter. The arcades are not uniform, and on the north side the piers change from a square with four semicircular shafts at the east end to the normal Perpendicular type of four shafts and four hollows further west. The southern arcade piers have thin triple shafts on each side and four diagonal hollows. The chapels followed, and the clerestory with east windows over the chancel arch was added last of all. There is a fine old low pitched roof. The stalls in the south transept may be as old as the 13th century. The bench ends there with Gothic panelling and fleur-de-lys poppy-heads may be Elizabethan. The font with quatrefoils on the bowl, heads on the underside, and panelling on the stem is of c1500. The communion rail is partly 18th century. The only pre-1800 monument is a truncated alabaster effigy of Sir John Warburton, d1575. In the churchyard is an 18th century baluster-type sundial.

Tower doorway at Great Budworth

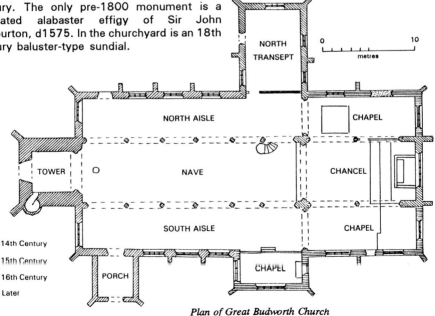

Plan of Great Budworth Church

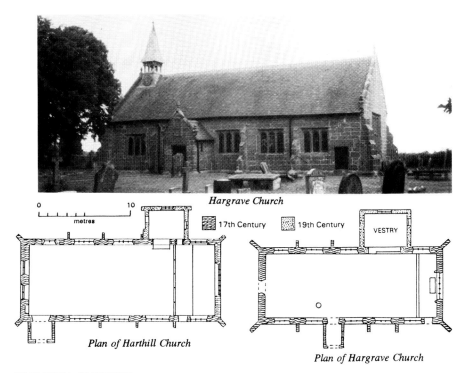

Hargrave Church

0   10
metres

▨ 17th Century   ▨ 19th Century

VESTRY

Plan of Harthill Church

Plan of Hargrave Church

GUILDEN SUTTON   *St John Baptist*   SJ 440686

In the small brick church of 1815, which has four bays with a pointed mullioned east window, is a font dated 1635 carved with one flower. The bell-turret is Victorian.

HANDLEY   *All Saints*   SJ 466579

The west tower has an inscription and the date 1512 on the west side. The rest is mostly of the rebuilding by James Harrison in 1853-5 except for the continuously moulded south doorway and the hammerbeam roof dated 1662 with fine corbels. A Norman doorway recorded here in 1849 was removed during the rebuilding.

HARGRAVE   *St Peter*   SJ 485622

The church is dated 1627 with an inscription referring to its construction by Sir Thomas Moulson, later Lord Mayor of London. It has mullioned windows with arched lights, the east window also having a transom. The hammerbeam roof has pendants. It appears that the building was also intended to be used as a school-house. In 1878-90 a big vestry was added and a ceiling inserted in 1774 was removed.

HARTHILL   *All Saints*   SJ 500552

The wide single chamber with mullioned windows with arched lights and a hammerbeam roof on brackets probably dates from 1609. A chapel existed here in 1280, and it is thought to have been timber framed until 1609. The clock turret is of 1862-3. The communion rail and a columnar sundial outside are 18th century.

HESWALL   *St Peter*   SJ 266812

The tower has an early 16th century upper stage with panelled battlements on a 14th century lower stage. It was originally at the west end of the nave, but the south aisle now lies beyond it as a result of a rebuilding in 1879 by Francis Doyle. He extended the church to the east and SE in 1893. The font is an 18th century baluster, and there is a similar sundial outside. In the tower are a late 17th century chandelier and monuments to John Glegg, d1619, and Katherine Glegg, d1666.

HIGH LEGH   *St Mary*   SJ 701841

The chapel now stands by an estate of new detached houses but originally served the demolished hall of 1782. The chapel is a brick building of c1581 with an aisle of 1836 which was given cross-gables by Butterfield in 1858. J. Oldrid Scott added the chancel in 1884. There are original timber piers inside.

HOLMES CHAPEL

St Luke   SJ 763673

A large timber framed medieval church with arcades of four bays with octagonal piers with eight thin rolls was encased in a brick shell in the early 18th century, leaving only the stone west tower exposed. There are entrances in the second and sixth bays and two tiers of windows which are round arched and segmental-arched respectively. The chancel is lower. Over the west door is a frieze dated 1623. The west and south galleries are dated 1705. The brass chandelier is of 1708.

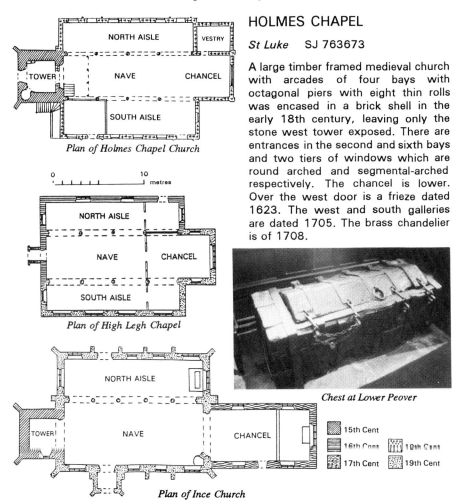

Plan of Holmes Chapel Church

Plan of High Legh Chapel

Chest at Lower Peover

Plan of Ince Church

15th Cent
16th Cent
17th Cent
18th Cent
19th Cent

Holmes Chapel Church

INCE   *St James*   SJ 450764

The chancel has a roof dated 1671 with moulded corbels and the walls and the communion rail are likely to be of about the same date. The tower is 15th century but the top belongs to the period of the rebuilding of the nave by Hodgkinson in 1854 when a Norman nave doorway was destroyed. There is a chandelier of 1724.

Ince Church

Lower Peover Church

KNUTSFORD   *St John Baptist*   SJ 753785

This brick church with stone dressings was built in 1741-4 by J. Garlive at a cost of £4,000, to replace an older building which had recently collapsed. It has a west tower and a nave and aisles of five bays with two tiers of arched windows. The building was lengthened eastwards in 1879. See photo on page 11.

KNUTSFORD   *St Cross*   SJ 756786.

In the church of 1880-1 designed by Paley and Austin is a small bronze relief of the Deposition of Christ in the Mannerist style. It is dated 1607 with the initials H. K.

LITTLE BUDWORTH   *St Peter*   SJ 598655

In 1790-1800 the church was entirely rebuilt except for the west tower of c1526. The Manchester merchant Ralph Kirkham left £1,000 towards the rebuilding. The pulpit and font are also of c1800. Inside is a 17th century Italian painting of the Entombment of Christ given to the church by one of the Egerton family.

Lower Whitley Church

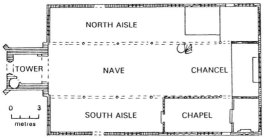

Plan of Lower Peover Church

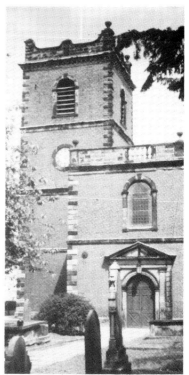

Knutsford Church

LOWER PEOVER   *St Oswald*   SJ 744743

Except for the west tower built, or more likely just repaired, in 1582, this is a black-and-white timber framed church. A chapel existed here in 1269 and the dug-out chest is of that period, but the present building appears to be 14th century. However it has been much altered, a south chapel being added c1610, a north chapel in 1624, and considerable work done by Salvin in 1852 when the aisles were made wider and given separate roofs. Salvin made the south chapel, rebuilt in brick during the 18th century, timber framed again. The pulpit with blank arches, the chapel screens, font cover, box pews and lectern are Jacobean. In the south chapel are monuments to Godfrey Shakerley, d1696, and Katherine Shakerley, 1725.

LOWER WHITLEY   *St Luke*   SJ 614789

This brick building with mullioned windows with arched lights and a splendid hammerbeam roof with large brackets with scrolls was built c1620 by Thomas Touchet. The polygonal apse dates from one of the 19th century restorations.

LYMM   *St Mary*   SJ 683868

In the church of 1850-2 by Dobson are an octagonal font of c1660, a pulpit dated 1623, and a probable Roman altar lying within a 14th century tomb recess. The 15th century nave and aisles were blown up with gunpowder prior to rebuilding.

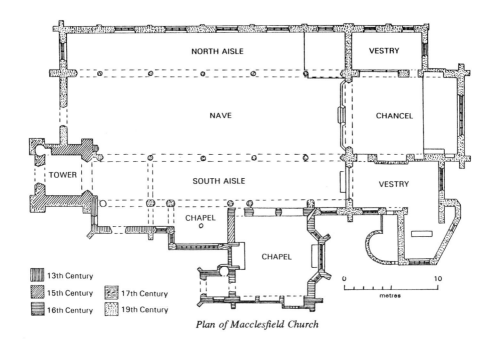

NORTH AISLE

VESTRY

NAVE

CHANCEL

TOWER

SOUTH AISLE

VESTRY

CHAPEL

CHAPEL

	13th Century		17th Century
	15th Century		
	16th Century		19th Century

0   10

metres

Plan of Macclesfield Church

MACCLESFIELD   *St Michael (formerly All Hallows)*   SJ 918738

Much of the large church is the work of Sir Arthur Blomfield in 1898-1901, replacing
a building of 1740 which was given a new east end in 1819. The present south aisle
corresponds to the original nave of the church consecrated in 1278. West of it is a
15th century tower with a tierceron vault with a large bell-rope hole. On the south
side of it is the Savage chapel built by Thomas Savage, Archbishop of York, in
1501-7. The chapel is of two bays and has to the south-west its own splendid three
storey porch like a small tower. The chapel west window is a relic of another chapel
to the east founded c1422 and rebuilt in 1620. The font is a fluted bowl on a thick
baluster and is of 1744. A chandelier of the same date was remodelled in 1822. In
the chancel are alabaster effigies of a knight of c1475, of Sir John Savage, d1495,
and his wife holding hands. Under arches between the Savage chapel and the
chancel are alabaster effigies of Sir John Savage, d1492, and John Savage, d1527.
On the chapel west wall is a brass depicting Roger Legh, d1506 with his sons and
inscriptions telling us that the pardon for five Paternosters, five Alves, and one
Creed is 26,000 years and 26 days. The figures of his wife and daughters are
missing. Next to it are recumbent effigies of Sir John Savage, d1597 and his wife,
erected c1635. By the chapel south wall is an effigy of a civilian of c1500 with the
torso left hidden and uncarved within the block, and alabaster effigies of Sir John
Savage, d1528, and his wife. In the south aisle is a semi-reclining effigy of Earl
Rivers, made in 1696 by William Stanton.

MACCLESFIELD FOREST   SJ 974722

The church lies among the moors 6km ESE of Macclesfield. It was built in 1673 but
was entirely rebuilt in 1834, then gaining a short saddle-back roofed west tower.

Brass of Roger Legh at Macclesfield

Porch-tower on the Savage Chapel at Macclesfield

Interior of Macclesfield Church

MALPAS   *St Oswald*   SJ 486472

At a glance the church exterior looks all of c1480-1520 with its battlements and pinnacles, the splendid two storey south porch, the clerestory of four light windows and the large chancel and aisle windows with panel tracery. The six bay arcades inside and the fine low pitched roof with numerous bosses are of that period too. Yet the shell of the building is in fact 14th century. Of that period are the tower base, the tower and chancel arches, the lower parts of the chancel with sedilia, a piscina and the north vestry doorway, plus a treasury underneath the east end allowed by a steep fall of the ground. Also 14th century are the lower parts of the aisle outer walls with four large cusped tomb recesses on the north side and a piscina in the south aisle, plus the eastern respond of the north arcade, showing that the original arcades were much lower. The piers have four shafts and four subsidiary diagonal shafts. The tower contains a vault with a ribs converging on a large hole for the bell-ropes. A spire was intended but never completed. There is a NE vestry of 1764, a brick structure with prominent quoins and a balustraded parapet.

The 15th century font has quatrefoils on the bowl, fleurons on the base and panelling on the stem. The south and north chapels (belonging respectively to the Brereton and Cholmondeley families) have screens with ornate inscriptions. The chancel and south chapel contain medieval stalls with faces on the arm rests. There are three misericords depicting two knights in combat, a mermaid, and a monster. There are box pews, one of which has a beam dated 1680 and there is an old chest with intricate iron scrolls. Above the chancel arch is a painting of St Peter's Denial of Christ, by Hayman, given in 1778. The 16th century glass in the north chapel is mostly foreign. In the nave is an incised slab depicting Urian Davenport, d1495, a rector of the church. In the south chapel are fine alabaster effigies of Randle Brereton and his wife, dating c1522. In the north chapel are effigies of Sir Hugh Cholmondeley and his wife. Against the tomb chest are kneeling children and a baby in swaddling clothes. In the south aisle are tablets to Bridget Kynaston, d1644 and John Stockton, d1700.

Malpas Church

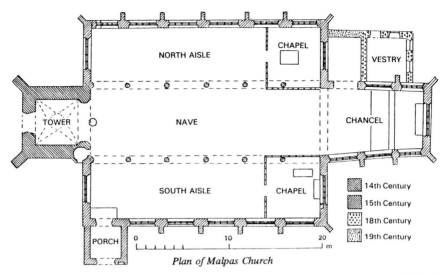

Plan of Malpas Church

14th Century
15th Century
18th Century
19th Century

Porch at Malpas

Marbury Church

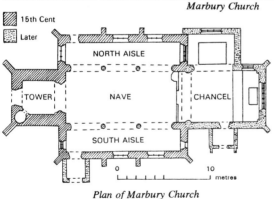

Plan of Marbury Church

Tower at Mellor

MARBURY   *St Michael*   SJ 560457

This is a 15th century church of red sandstone set beside a mere. The nave has arcades of three low arches on each side and a clerestory, battlements and pinnacles. The west tower has diagonal buttresses and two bands of fleurons. At the top it has eight pinnacles springing from gargoyles. The mid-wall pinnacles are set diagonally. The chancel was rebuilt c1822. It was remodelled by Douglas and Fordham in 1891, when new battlements were put on the aisles and the brick porch was refaced with stone. The medieval pulpit has crocketted ogee panels.

Marton Church

NORTH AISLE · CHAPEL · TOWER · NAVE · CHANCEL · SOUTH AISLE · CHAPEL · 0 — 10 metres

Plan of Marton Church

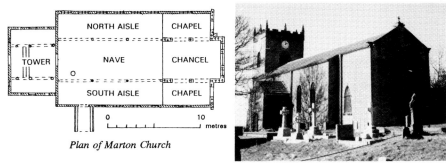

Mellor Church

MARTON   *St James and St Paul*   SJ 850680

Marton is a timber-framed 14th century church with a west tower (actually a shingled turret) having a lean-to roofed aisle around the north, west, and south sides like some of the wooden towers in Essex. The nave has arcades of three bays. The octagonal piers have arched braces both longitudinally and transversely. The original windows were of two lights; the present ones of three lights date from a restoration by Derrick in 1850, whilst Butterfield tidied up some of the tower timbers in 1871. There are traces of old wall paintings on the west wall. From an 18th century reredos has come the painting of Moses and Aaron holding Commandment tables. The pulpit is of 1620. There are two damaged effigies of 14th century knights.

MELLOR   *St Thomas*   SJ 982889

The church lies high up with wide views to the west, north and south. It was rebuilt in the early 19th century except for the 16th century west tower. From 1678 the church became a chapel-of-ease to Glossop, but it regained full parochial status in 1775. Inside are a 14th century pulpit with traceried panels which is carved out of a single block of wood, and a Norman font with crude carvings of a man on horseback, two animals and what looks like a seated child. These two treasures were removed from the church in the 1820s but brought back in 1884. See p12.

MIDDLEWICH   *St Michael*   SJ 704663

The narrow eastern bays of the arcades with round piers and single-stepped arches are reset Norman work. Otherwise the church is mostly of c1480-1520 and is large and embattled, with pinnacles. The western parts of the arcades have octagonal piers with fleurons on the capitals. Because of a roadway which passed to the SW the tower lies west of the north side, and the south aisle was given a canted west bay. The east end of the aisle (which formed a Lady chapel) is canted also, supposedly for symmetry's sake. On the north side of the chancel is the 16th century Kinderton chapel which was wider than the north aisle until the latter was rebuilt in the restoration of 1857-60 by Joseph Clarke. The nave has a ceiled roof dated 1621. The screen of the former north chapel is dated 1632, and the chancel screen and stalls incorporate Flemish 16th and 17th century panels. The south chapel contains a defaced stone effigy and the north chapel contains two 17th century memorial tablets. The church was much damaged during the Civil War, when a battle was fought in and around it. The Royalists were defeated, about thirty being killed and five hundred being taken prisoner.

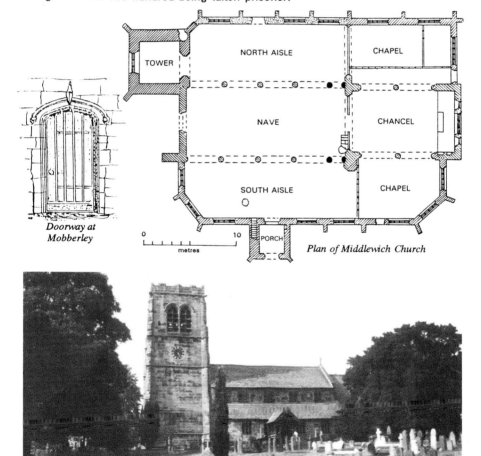

Doorway at Mobberley

Plan of Middlewich Church

Mobberley Church

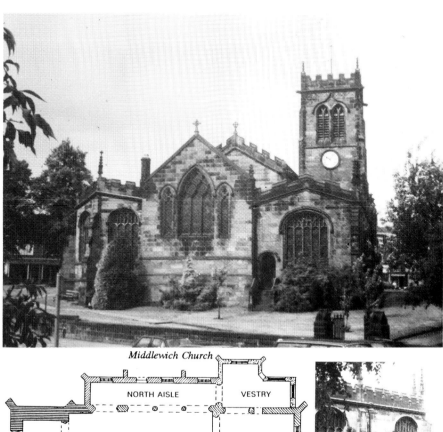

Middlewich Church

Plan of Mobberley Church

▨	14th Century
▨	15th Century
▤	16th Century
▦	Later & Modern

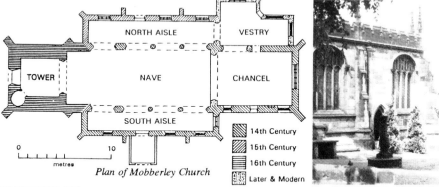

Middlewich Church

MOBBERLEY   *St Wilfred*   SJ 791803

The arcades have three 14th century bays and an extra bay with fleurons on the capitals which was added c1530 to link up with the big west tower then newly built. The aisles are quite narrow. The chancel has a piscina of c1300 but the chancel arch and the east end are the work of J.S.Crowther in 1889. Against the chancel arch is a very fine screen dated 1500. Above is a ceilure. The nave has a low pitched medieval roof with big cambered beams and panelling and there are wall paintings of St Christopher and other figures now too worn to be recognised. The tower contains a gallery dated 1683. There are fragments of old glass in the south aisle windows. The tiny font is Georgian. A painted board shows a shroud and is said to be dated 1665 with the names of Elizabeth and Nathaniel Robinson.

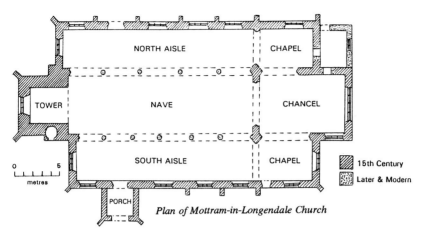

Plan of Mottram-in-Longendale Church

MOTTRAM-IN-LONGENDALE   *St Michael*   SJ 997953

This large late-medieval church lies on a hilltop. The west tower is thought to be of the 1480s. The aisles have three light windows with cusped heads, stepped and without tracery. The arcades, of six bays on the south, and of five wider bays on the north, were rebuilt in 1854 and a new clerestory added in place of a lower original one. The chancel is flanked by two chapels and has a transomed five-light east window. The interior was thoroughly restored in 1854 by Shellard leaving only a big brass chandelier of 1755, an ancient tub font, and a painting of Moses and Aaron with texts, now over the chancel arch, but formerly part of a reredos. In the south chapel are two defaced 15th century stone effigies. The chancel has an almost totally defaced incised slab of John Pycton, d1517, a rector of the church, and in the north chapel is a semi-reclining effigy of Reginald Bretland, d1703.

Mottram-in-Longendale Church

Nantwich Church

NANTWICH   *St Mary*   SJ 653524

Until the 17th century St Mary's ranked only as a chapel-of-ease to Acton, yet it is a large cruciform church (only surpassed in size by the monastic churches of the county) with many fine details mostly of the 14th century. The crossing piers have springers for a vault which was never built. Above is an octagonal belfry. The Lady Chapel (now a vestry) beyond the north transept was also intended to be vaulted. The chancel has a lierne-vault and has ogee arches over the sedilia and piscina and side windows with crocketted gables. The seven light east window is in the Perpendicular style rather than Decorated like the rest. It is uncertain whether it is a replacement or simply represents the last effort of a long single building campaign. On the north side of the chancel is a contemporary treasury. The chantry endowed in 1405 is assumed to have occupied the south transept which also has a Perpendicular end window. In 1461 there were six chantry priests serving in the church. The nave arcades are of four bays and above is a clerestory of eight windows on each side. The vaulted south porch is 15th century. The church was damaged during the Civil War and was used as a prison. It fell into a great state of decay in the 18th century but was restored by Sir George Gilbert Scott in 1854-61, the west front being mostly his work. He also rebuilt the north aisle, but with the old materials, including buttresses with the arms of the Mainwaring family.

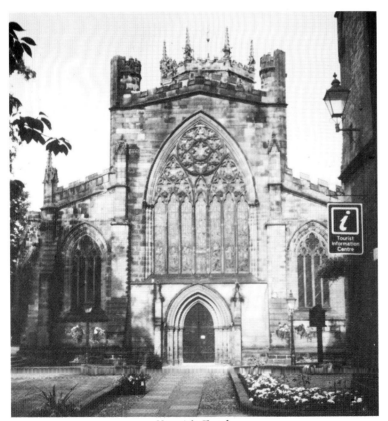

Nantwich Church

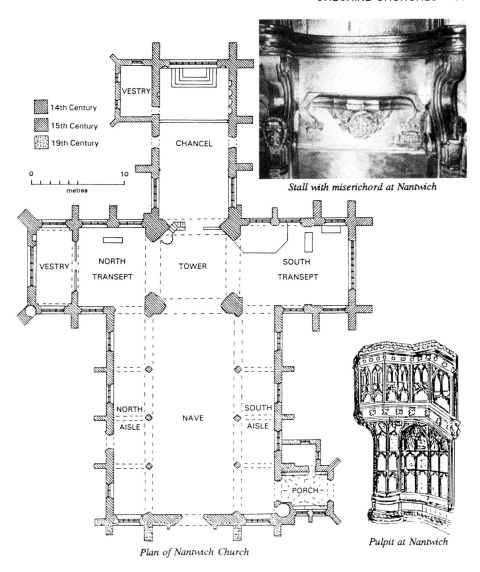

14th Century
15th Century
19th Century

0   10
metres

VESTRY

CHANCEL

Stall with miserichord at Nantwich

VESTRY

NORTH
TRANSEPT

TOWER

SOUTH
TRANSEPT

NORTH
AISLE

NAVE

SOUTH
AISLE

PORCH

Plan of Nantwich Church

Pulpit at Nantwich

The chancel has contemporary stalls with twenty misericords carved with motifs such as a woman beating her husband with a ladle, the Devil pulling a nun's mouth open, Samson and the Lion, Virgin and Unicorn, skinning a stag, a pelican, a fox pretending to be dead, a nun reading, St George and the Dragon, a mermaid, a pair of wrestlers, and several dragons. One crossing pier has a stone pulpit built into it and there is also a wooden pulpit dated 1601. One chancel window retains some contemporary glass. In the south transept is a damaged alabaster effigy thought to be of Sir David Craddock, d1384. There is also a large and splendid tomb transferred here from the destroyed church at Wybunbury with recumbent effigies of Sir Thomas Smith, d1614, and his wife Anne Brereton. See photos on pages 9 & 13.

Nether Alderley Church

Nether Alderley Church

NESTON   *St Mary and St Helen*   SJ 292775

In 1874-5 J. Francis Doyle rebuilt the main body of the church, which included four bay Norman arcades with 18th century patching, and heightened the 14th century tower which has reused Norman material in the lower stages. Squinches show that a spire existed or was intended. The plaque dated 1697 refers to repairs, perhaps to the main body of the church, rather than the tower upon which it is mounted. In the church are a 15th century font, a floriated cross slab to a 14th century priest, and fragments of two Saxon crosses, including part of a circular head with cable moulding and knotwork, and parts of a shaft with fighting figures, a winged figure and an ecclesiastic. In the churchyard is a Georgian baluster-type sundial.

NETHER ALDERLEY   *St Mary*   SJ 842761

The west tower, the three bay arcades, the fine roofs, and much else are 15th century but there are 14th century doorways to the west and south. On the south side is the 17th century Stanley family pew, a two storied addition, and on the north side is a dormer window of the same period. The chancel was rebuilt in 1856 by Cuffley and Starkey. Only two out of an original set of four heads survive on the 14th century font. The only pre-1800 monument is that of Rev Edward Shipton, d1630. Beside the churchyard entrance is a mullioned windowed school of 1693.

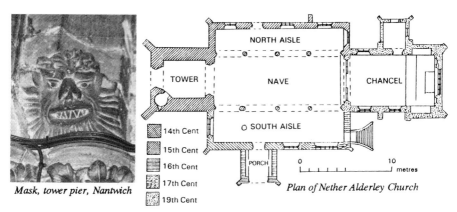

Mask, tower pier, Nantwich

14th Cent
15th Cent
16th Cent
17th Cent
19th Cent

NORTH AISLE

TOWER

NAVE

CHANCEL

SOUTH AISLE

PORCH

0   10
⊥ ⊥ ⊥ ⊥ ⊥ ⊥   ⊥ metres

Plan of Nether Alderley Church

Neston Church

NORTHWICH   *St Helen*   SJ 665739

The church of St Helen at Witton originally ranked only as a chapel-of-ease to Great Budworth. The tower arch and the arcade piers with four semi-circles with hollows in the diagonals are 14th century. Most of the rest is of c1500-25 when the north arcade was moved northwards to make a wider nave, and a chancel arch removed. Its southern respond still survives, being once hidden by a screen with a loft reached by a stair opposite. Chapels were added on either side of the chancel, and the splendid ceiling with large and small bosses was put up. A polygonal east apse then added was rebuilt in 1861, much of the church being renewed then and in other restorations of 1842 and 1884. During this period the north aisle was widened.

Apart from the arch, the tower is the work of the mason Thomas Hunter and has two decorative bands. The only old furnishings are a screen in the vestry with a top beam dated 1641 and a 14th century reredos in the south chapel. See photo p10.

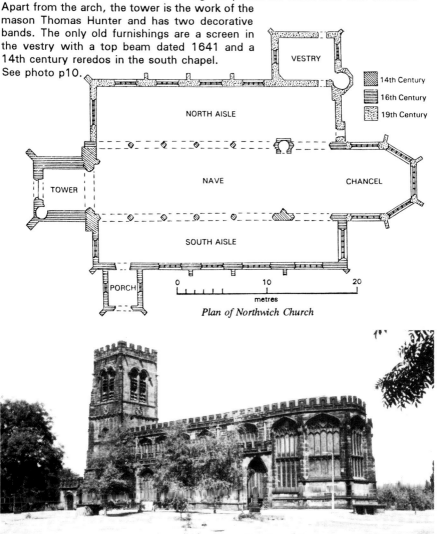

Plan of Northwich Church

Northwich Church

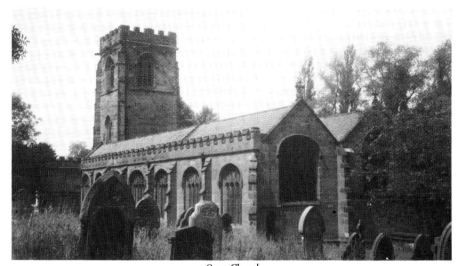

Over Church

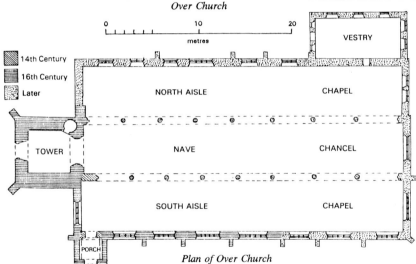

Plan of Over Church

OVER   *St Chad*   SJ 650651

The church lies alone at the south end of Over, which is now part of Winsford. The east end is a lengthening of 1926 but incorporates a reset 14th century east window with reticulated tracery. Until then the south arcade had six arches and the north arcade five. The west tower is of 1543, part of a general rebuilding by Hugh Starkey, gentleman usher to Henry VIII, whose tomb, with a brass on top, lies in a recess in an original section of the chancel north wall. The church was heavily restored by Toulon in 1870. The aisles are wider than the nave but the north aisle only attained its present width when it was rebuilt in 1904. The south side has four and five light windows and battlements and a two storey porch with an ornamented stoup. The porch inner doorway is 14th century. One reset window in the north aisle has fragments of old glass. In the chancel is a Saxon stone decorated with interlace.

Over Peover Church

OVER PEOVER   *St Laurence*   SJ 772736

The church lies in the middle of an estate far from any public road. The main body
is a brick structure of 1811 by William Turner, but it has a west tower of 1739 with
round windows, a 15th century south chapel of two bays, and a classical style north
chapel of c1650. The north chapel has an east pediment and lunette windows high
up and its ceiling has a coat of arms in the middle. It was built to contain a
monument to Philip Mainwaring, d1647, and contains a suit of armour of about that
period. Other monuments include alabaster effigies thought to be of John
Mainwaring, d1410, and his wife, alabaster effigies of Randle Mainwaring, d1456,
and his wife, incised alabaster slabs in the south chapel to Philip Mainwaring,
d1573, and Sir John Mainwaring, d1586, and their wives, plus a painted panel to
William Littleboys, d1624. The font and the fragments of old glass in the south
chapel are 15th century. The pulpit is Jacobean.

PLEMSTALL   *St Peter*   SJ 456701

The church is mostly 15th century and has a six bay north arcade, a hammerbeam
roof, a window on the south side with panel tracery and an original studded door.
The Georgian tower overlapping the joint between the nave and aisle dates from
1826. A vestry of that date has been demolished. Most of the fine woodwork is the
work of the Rev Toogood, incumbent from 1907 to 1946, but the parclose screen
has an early 16th century linenfold dado. The font is probably 17th century, and
there is a three decker pulpit dated 1722. A pew with a canopy on twisted columns
is dated 1697. One south window contains some old glass. A painted inscription
refers to benefactions from 1660 onwards. The monuments include a painted 17th
century heraldic tablet, and a tomb chest with a skeleton outside the church to
Elizabeth Hurleston, d1727. In the churchyard is an 18th century baluster sundial.

POTT SHRIGLEY *St Christopher*

SJ 945792

Originally a chantry chapel, and only made a parish church in the mid 16th century, much of this building was erected from funds left by Geoffrey Downes in 1492. The tower with three original bells and the aisles are certainly of that period. However the very unusual trefoil shaped pier of the two bay north arcade may be a relic of an older chapel. There are fine old roofs in the nave and chancel. There are box pews, an 18th century baluster font and the east window has fragments of medieval glass.

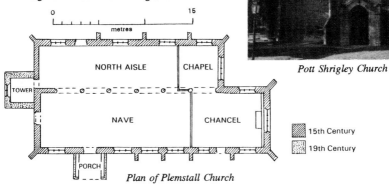

Pott Shrigley Church

0 ⊢ ⊣ ⊢ ⊣ ⊢ ⊣ 15
metres

NORTH AISLE   CHAPEL

TOWER

NAVE   CHANCEL

PORCH

▨ 15th Century
▦ 19th Century

Plan of Plemstall Church

Plemstall Church

PRESTBURY   *St Peter*   SJ 901769

The church has 13th century arcades, the south piers being quatrefoils with fillets and the north piers being alternately round and octagonal, although the responds are all the same. Half-figures of Apostles were painted on the spandrels in 1719. The chancel has a late 13th century window with triple shafts dividing the lights. It now looks into an extension. The tympanum of the chancel doorway with a trellis pattern is a reset piece of c1200. The south aisle has mullioned windows of 1612 and a 14th century doorway. The north aisle was rebuilt wider in 1739-41 and remodelled in 1879-85 by Sir George Gilbert Scott, who put in the present east window in the chancel. The west tower with clasping buttreses was built in the 1480s. It has a Jacobean screen under its arch with a balcony of 1637 above. The classical chapel screen is dated 1739 and the chancel screen is of the same period. The communion rail in the Legh chapel is 17th century, as are the pews in the nave west end. The chancel has a chandelier of 1712; the grander one in the nave is of 1814. The pulpit is dated 1607. There are incised slabs in the chancel to Reginald Legh, d1482, Robert Downes, d1495, and his wife, and Edward Warren, d1558. In the south aisle is an incised slab to Jasper Warren, d1592 and a late 17th century brass inscription.

Prestbury Church

Norman chapel at Prestbury

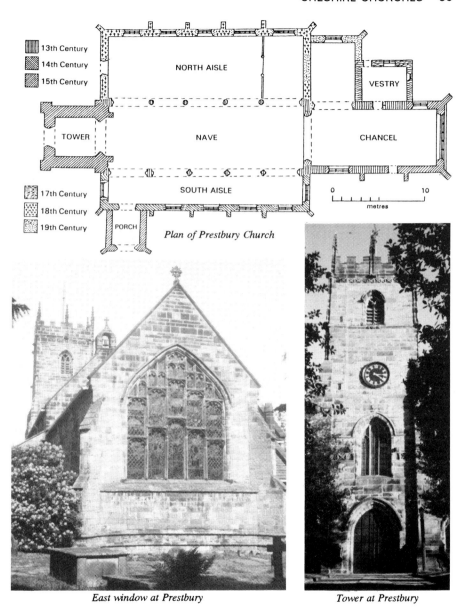

13th Century
14th Century
15th Century

17th Century
18th Century
19th Century

NORTH AISLE

VESTRY

TOWER

NAVE

CHANCEL

SOUTH AISLE

0   10
metres

PORCH

Plan of Prestbury Church

East window at Prestbury

Tower at Prestbury

Close to Prestbury church are a fragment of a Saxon cross in a glass case and a Norman chapel which was later taken over as the burial place of the Davenports of Henbury. The chapel is shown on a sketch of 1592 as having a roofless nave and an east apse which was probably vaulted. It was mostly rebuilt in 1747 and the only original part is the west doorway with two orders of columns and with rows of heads, chevrons, and pellets on the arches. There is a tympanum showing Christ in a halo held by angels and above is a row of seven figures.

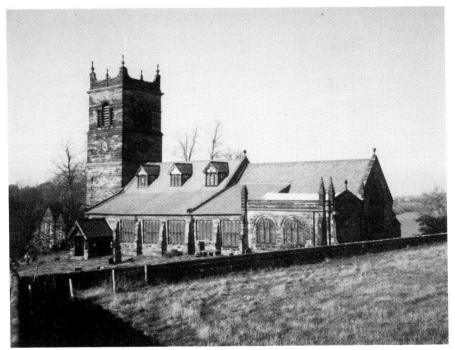

Rostherne Church

ROSTHERNE   *St Mary*   SJ 743837

The church is attractively placed above the mere and is reached from the road through a 17th century turning lych-gate. The west tower of 1742-4 replaces one of 1533 which collapsed through neglect. As early as 1592 as it "wanteth pointing and leade". The chancel and north vestry are of 1888 by Sir Arthur Blomfield. The nave and aisles with uncusped arched lights to the mullioned windows appear to be all 16th century externally, although the south arcade and the north doorway and the aisle east window now looking into the vestry are 14th century, and the north arcade has round 13th century piers. There are several monuments of note of late date plus a badly mutilated effigy of a 13th century knight and a tablet with a putto holding a portrait medallion to John Egerton, d1738.

RUNCORN   *All Saints*   SJ 511833

The church lies by the river and was entirely rebuilt by Salvin in 1847-9. Until then it had a low embattled 14th century tower with diagonal buttresses and a 13th century nave and aisle. Among numerous monuments to the Brookes of Norton Priory is a tablet to Thomas, d1737.

SALTERSFORD   OJ 304/66

Hidden away up in the hills 7km NE of Macclesfield is the lonely Jenkin Chapel of 1733, with a short saddleback-roofed west tower added in 1754-5. Original are the square windows and the west gallery, the box pews, and the two-decker pulpit.

Jenkin Chapel at Saltersford

SANDBACH   *St Mary*   SJ 759608

The famous 9th century crosses lie away from the church in the middle of the village and are cared for by English Heritage. The north cross depicts the Transfiguration, the Nativity, the Crucifixion, The Passion, and the Signs of the Evangelists. The south cross has various figures and what is probably a Resurrection. Fragments of other Saxon crosses and two broken medieval coffin lids lie beside the church.

The church itself was a major 15th century building until rebuilt by Sir George Gilbert Scott in 1847-9. He left some walling on the south side, parts of the arcades, roofs dated 1661 and a font of 1667 with leaves. The tower appears to reproduce the original one and has arches to the north and south and ogival arches over the double belfry windows. Scott made the original chancel and its flanking chapels into the east part of his nave and aisles and added a new chancel beyond.

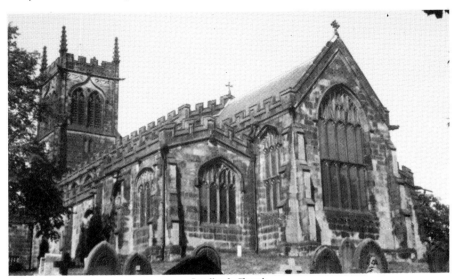

Sandbach Church

Shocklach Church

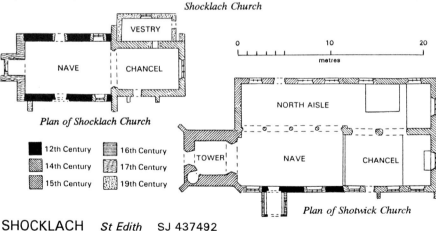

Plan of Shocklach Church

■ 12th Century	▦ 16th Century	
▨ 14th Century	▨ 17th Century	
▨ 15th Century	▓ 19th Century	

Plan of Shotwick Church

SHOCKLACH   *St Edith*   SJ 437492

The nave is Norman and there is an original south doorway with chevrons, rope ornament, and lozenges. The chancel is 14th century, the east window, priest's doorway, chancel arch with supporting buttresses, and the nave north doorway being of that period. The baptistry squeezed in between two west buttresses bearing the arms of the Breretons of Shocklach and the Egertons of Ridley is of the period after the Egertons inherited the manor, purchased by the Breretons in 1572. The pulpit is of 1687 and the font in its present form is of about the same time. The communion rail and the fine nave ceiling decorated with rosettes are 18th century.

Shotwick Church

SHOTWICK   *St Michael*   SJ 337719

The Norman south doorway with scalloped capitals on the shafts and a random chequer pattern on the arch is very worn. The chancel and north chapel are 14th century, both having reticulated tracery in their east windows, although the priest's doorway looks as if it may date from c1200. The north aisle is late 15th century except for a short section of 14th century masonry in the west wall, and the west tower is of c1500 whilst the plain mullioned south windows are late 16th or 17th century. Much of the old woodwork in the church is said to have been transferred in 1812 from a church at Chester. It includes a 15th century studded door, a Georgian three-decker pulpit, a churchwardens' pew dated 1709 on a canopy carried by two balusters, a 17th century communion rail with turned balusters, and box pews. The brass chandelier is late 18th century. The north chapel east window contains fragments of original glass including an Annunciation.

Siddington Church

SIDDINGTON   *All Saints*   SJ 846708

This was a medieval timber framed building and had an east window with glass dated 1513. Original are the south porch and the chancel with two narrow bays with timber wall-shafts, arched braces, and herringbone bracing. The nave is now whitened brick with a half-timbered effect painted on it, and the window tracery is of c1820. The screen survives and from its loft parapet may have come the tracery panels in the chancel east wall. The pulpit is of 1633.

SOMERFORD   *All Saints*   SJ 815648

The brick chapel of 1725 with a chequer-pattern on the walls, arched windows, projecting quoins, a cupola, and a west doorway with a moulded surround, served the hall of the same period, now demolished except for one wing and the stables.

STOAK   *St Lawrence*   SJ 424734

Except for its roof the nave was rebuilt in 1827 by George Edgecumbe. The small chancel is 15th century. The west gallery incorporates panels from the dado of an early 16th century screen of Welsh type. The pulpit and the communion rail with twisted balusters are late 17th century. There are many painted heraldic 17th century tablets plus a large marble cartouche to Henry Bunbury, d1668.

STOCKPORT   *St Mary*   SJ 894904

The west tower and spacious nave are the work of Lewis Wyatt in 1813-17 but the chancel, although much restored outside, is 14th century. It has a double piscina, sedilia with crocketted gables on the south side and on the north a three centred arch containing a very mutilated effigy of rector Ralph de Vernon, d1004. The earliest of many other monuments is the tablet to William Wright, d1753. Old prints suggest that the church had a south aisle and west window of the 14th century. The original tower, 14th century but mostly rebuilt in 1612-16 and rebuilt again in 1810, stood west of the north aisle.

Stoak Church

STOCKPORT   *St Peter*   SJ 894904

This church was built in 1768 at the expense of William Wright, d1770, whose monument lies inside it. It is a brick building with arched windows and a west tower with an octagonal top stage and cap. The chancel was added in 1888.

Medieval chancel at St Mary's at Stockport

Swettenham Church

SWETTENHAM   *St Peter*   SJ 801672

Much of the church, including the brick west tower, the chequered brickwork of the chancel, the Capesthorne chapel with its oval windows, the segment headed north window, the communion rail and the oldest of the two fonts are of c1717-22. However the chancel turns out inside to be a medieval timber framed structure, the imitation Norman north arcade is of 1846, and the south windows are of the 1860s.

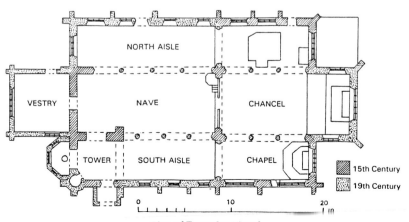

Plan of Tarporley Church

TABLEY   *St Peter*   SJ 725777

In 1927-9 the chapel built in 1675-8 by the Cheshire historian Sir Peter Leicester was removed from its position beside the collapsing old hall to its present site west of Tabley House. It is a brick building with windows having arched lights and transoms. The east window has two transoms and a gable of convex curves. Sir Frederick Leicester added the thin west tower c1720. Inside are a segmental plaster vault and wooden panelling. The pulpit has a tester and an hourglass. Other interesting furnishings include a west screen, the communion rail with twisted balusters, pews with balls on the ends and some pieces of Dutch glass.

TARPORLEY   *St Helen*   SJ 554625

Except for the 15th century north and south chapels, the exterior was mostly renewed in the 1860s and 70s by J. Crowther. Until then the chancel, south aisle and south porch were mostly 14th century work. The tower lies west of the south aisle, leaving space at the west end of the nave for a baptistry of 1931-2 designed by Sir Percy Warrington. The arcades inside, of four bays for the nave and aisles, and of three for the chancel and chapels, plus the chancel arch, are 15th century. The furnishings are not old except for the gates of the iron screen, said to be 16th century work from Siena. A monument of 1698 has effigies of Jane Done, d1622, her sister Mary Crewe, d1690, and the latter's granddaughter, d1674. There is also a reclining effigy of Sir John Crewe, d1711. There are late 17th century tablets with busts of Sir John Done, d1629, and John Crewe, d1670. See photo on page 8.

Tarporley Church

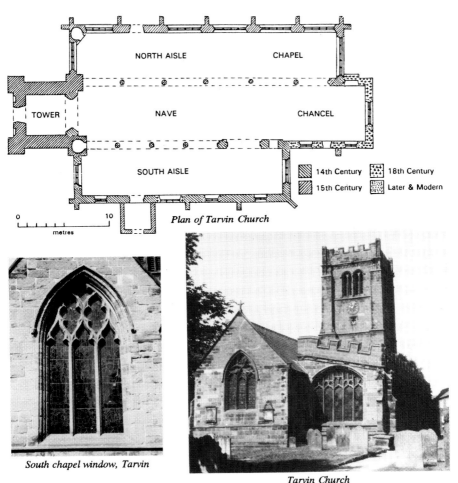

Plan of Tarvin Church

NORTH AISLE   CHAPEL

TOWER   NAVE   CHANCEL

SOUTH AISLE

14th Century   18th Century
15th Century   Later & Modern

0 ——————— 10
metres

South chapel window, Tarvin

Tarvin Church

TARVIN   *St Andrew*   SJ 492670

Of the 14th century are the south aisle with its four bay arcade and original roof of closely spaced arch-braced trusses plus the south chapel with its windows and one arch and a panelled opening for a monument towards what was originally part of the chancel but which later became the east end of the nave. The chapel has an original screen but the stained glass in the windows was removed c1600 by John Bruen, the chapel proprietor, because of the "many superstitious images". The aisle has an 18th century Venetian window and others of the 19th century. The tower arch is 14th century, although the tower itself with clasping west buttresses is 15th century and has a west doorway flanked by niches and crowned by an ogival gable and a quatrefoil frieze. The embattled north aisle with an arcade of five arches on short octagonal piers is also 15th century, and with it goes the font with quatrefoils and a panelled stem. The splendid nave roof with hammerbeams is dated 1650. In the 18th century this roof and that in the aisle were hidden by a plaster ceilings (now removed), and the 14th century chancel was rebuilt. The saints, and reliefs on the reredos are Flemish work of c1500. There is a late 18th century chandelier.

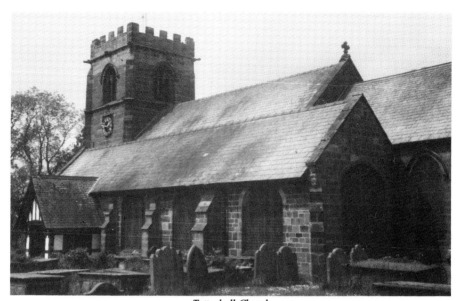

Tattenhall Church

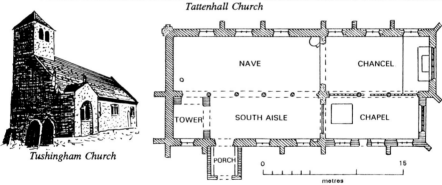

Tushingham Church

Plan of Thornton-le-Moors Church

TATTENHALL   *St Alban*   SJ 486585

The church was entirely rebuilt in 1869-70 by Douglas except for the 15th century west tower. One window contains 14th century stained glass depicting two saints. There is a particularly fine brass chandelier of 1755.

THORNTON-LE-MOORS   *St Mary*   SJ 442747

The church is overshadowed by a huge oil refinery. The south aisle with its big doorway and two-light windows, and the originally undivided nave and chancel with an east window with reticulated tracery are all 14th century. The south chapel, and the chancel south windows and hammer-beam roof, plus the tower inserted in the west end of the south aisle, are of c1500-30. The chapel east window and the nave west window and perhaps the chancel north windows are 17th century. The arch to the chapel is 19th century. The fluted font is 17th century. The communion rail with twisted balusters is dated 1695. There is a door of 1725. There are several painted heraldic memorial tablets dating from 1634 to 1687. See photo page 76.

Thornton-le-Moors Church

TILSTON   *St Mary*   SJ 457506

The church was much restored in 1877 but the tower is 15th century, the north chapel (although it looks earlier) is of 1659, and the north and south doorways and parts of the jambs of the straight headed windows are late medieval, or perhaps represent the rebuilding of 1689-91 with money left by the London merchant John Dod. The communion rail is dated 1677, and the pulpit is plain 18th century work.

TUSHINGHAM   *St Chad*   SJ 528463

The old church lying in the fields SE of the church of 1862 is a brick building of 1689-91 partly paid for by the London merchant John Dod. There are straight headed two light windows on the sides, a round arched east window, and a narrow pyramidal roofed west tower. Above the tie-beams are openwork panels with complex star shapes. The 17th century font looks like it may have been carved from a bedpost. Woodwork of note includes the three decker pulpit, the dado of the screen, the benches and a pair of family pews. See page 75.

WALLASEY   *St Hilary*   SJ 296928

The church lay in Claremount Road, east of Wallasey Village, but has vanished except for a tower with a 13th century lower stage with blocked arches to the west and north, and a top stage of the 1520s with arched uncusped lights to the bell-openings. A building of 1760 was rebuilt by W. & J. Hay in 1858-9 after being accidentally burnt in 1857. Of the 12th century church nothing remained except a few loose stones. A Norman font turned out in 1760 lay in the rectory garden until it was returned to the church in 1834. It was turned out again in 1856 and later taken to the new church at Poulton. See plan on page 78.

Tilston Church

WARBURTON

St Werburgh

SJ 697896

The old church in the village has a brick east tower dated 1711 with a hearse house east of it. The west wall and part of the south wall are of stone with the date 1645. The timber framed north side of the church and the timber piers inside are of uncertain but probably medieval date. The font is dated 1603 and the pulpit with blank arches goes with it. The three sided communion rail may be later. The bench inside it is said to have been inserted in 1857 to seat the choir.

Old Church at Warburton

Wervin Chapel

WARMINGHAM

St Leonard   SJ 709611

The west tower of dark brick with stone dressings and prominent quoins is of 1715. The main body of the church was timber framed until rebuilt in 1870 by Hussey. There is a monument in the Rococo style to William Vernon, d1732.

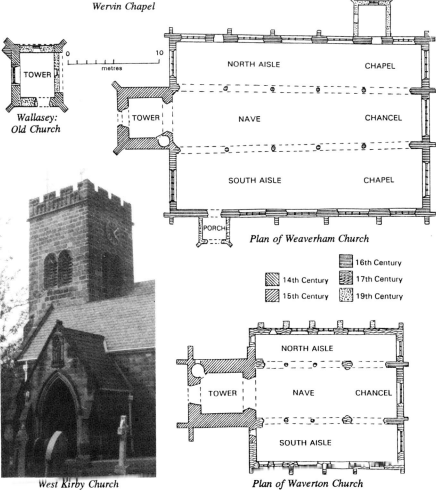

Wallasey: Old Church

TOWER

NORTH AISLE   CHAPEL

NAVE   CHANCEL

SOUTH AISLE   CHAPEL

PORCH

Plan of Weaverham Church

14th Century
15th Century
16th Century
17th Century
19th Century

West Kirby Church

NORTH AISLE

TOWER   NAVE   CHANCEL

SOUTH AISLE

Plan of Waverton Church

WAVERTON   *St Peter*   SJ 462633

The 15th century west tower has a fine doorway with decorated spandrels, a figure and shields above, and a window and recessed pyramidal roof of the 19th century. The chancel has late medieval timber framing. The clerestory and south doorway are probably 16th century, but they could be as late as the nave roof, which is dated 1635. The aisle roofs are of the same period. See photos on pages 9 & 10.

WEAVERHAM   *St Mary*   SJ 616743

The large west tower is said to have been begun before 1485. The rest, an aisled and embattled building with five bay arcades, is probably of c1520-40. The layout is irregular, with the main body noticeably becoming narrower towards the east end whilst the south aisle becomes wider there. The north aisle has a fine low-pitched roof. There is contemporary linenfold panelling around the altar. A south porch erected in 1852 was replaced by a larger one when the church was restored in 1877. Parts of a screen of c1530 and a three decker pulpit of 1774 are incorporated in pews. The parclose screens are of 1636. The font has a 13th century shaft and a later medieval bowl. The brass chandelier is 18th century.

WERVIN   SJ 422714

Just two fragments remain of the east wall of a chapel of uncertain date.

WEST KIRBY   *St Bridget*   SJ 208864

The church has a chancel which inclines to the north. It and much else was rebuilt in 1869-70 by Kelly and Edwards and a north porch was added in 1876. Some 14th century masonry including a trefoil-headed doorway survives in the north chapel and vestry and the chancel. Until the rebuilding the Norman arcade respond now lying in the museum formed part of the church. The tower with panelled battlements is early 16th century and some old parts remain in the north aisle.

Weaverham Church

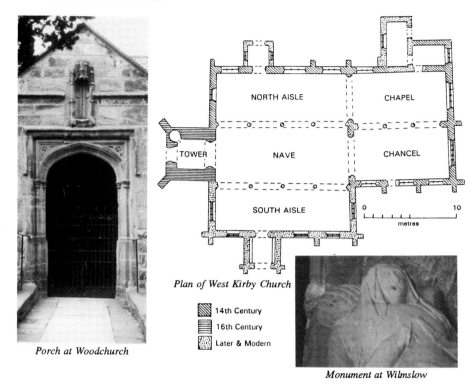

Plan of West Kirby Church

▨ 14th Century
▤ 16th Century
▨ Later & Modern

Porch at Woodchurch

Monument at Wilmslow

WHITEGATE   *St Mary*   SJ 628694

Lord Delamere had the church rebuilt by Douglas in 1874-5. Older relics are the south doorway of a brick building of 1728 with a west tower and east apse, and the octagonal timber piers of the original late medieval timber framed church.

WILMSLOW   *St Bartholomew*   SJ 848814

Of a 14th century church there remain the north and south doorways and the nave arcades with octagonal piers. A west tower was added c1490 and then in 1522 Henry Trafford, the rector, rebuilt the chancel. About the same time chapels were added and the nave clerestory with mullioned windows with uncusped arched lights. The chancel has the Hawthorne family pew of 1700 on the south side and was given a clerestory in 1898 by Bodley and Garner. The organ chamber was added during the restoration of 1862-3 by Brakspear, and Crowther in 1878 added the NE vestry and the south porch, and replaced the tower battlements and pinnacles. The family pew and two north aisle windows have fragments of old glass, and the chancel and parclose screens are partly old. On the chancel floor is a brass with figures of Robert Booth, d1460, and his wife, and in the north aisle are defaced effigies of Henry Trafford, d1537 and Humphrey Newton, d1536 and his wife.

WINCLE   *St Michael*   SJ 959662

A chapel built here in 1630 was given a west tower c1820. Apart from the tower it was entirely rebuilt in 1882 by Leonard Witts.

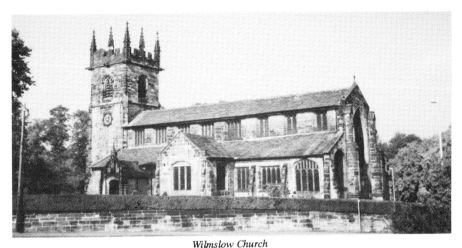

Wilmslow Church

14th Century
15th Century
16th Century
17th Century
Later & Modern

VESTRY

NORTH AISLE

CHAPEL

TOWER

NAVE

CHANCEL

SOUTH AISLE

CHAPEL

0   15
metres

*Plan of
Wilmslow Church*

WOODCHURCH *Holy Cross* SJ 276869

Not much now remains of the 12th century nave, a wide south aisle with a four bay arcade with octagonal piers being added in the 14th century, and a north aisle being added as recently as 1964. Some 17th century material is reset in the north aisle and the east and south-east windows of the south aisle are of that period. The south aisle was rebuilt in the 16th century, and a porch then added. This porch contains some fragments of old glass, has a niche for a statue over an outer arch with a square headed outer frame, and is approached by a flagged path flanked by yews. The 14th century west tower was given heavy diagonal buttresses in 1675. The chancel is dated 1584 but looks 14th century whilst the NE window is probably reset Norman work. The vestry was added in 1766. The octagonal 15th century font has angel corbels and the emblems of the Passion on the stem. In the chancel are four traceried medieval bench ends with poppy-heads, and three painted wooden panels commemorating Mary Ball, d1680, Mary Hockenhull, d1681, and William Hockenhull, d1698.

WRENBURY   *St Margaret*   SJ 594487

In 1488 Richard Cholmondley gave money towards rebuilding what was then a chapel-of-ease to Acton. The short west tower, and the wide nave and narrow aisles with arcades of five bays, a clerestory, and an original camber tie-beam roof with bosses, are of about that time or only slightly later. The tower west doorway has shields in the spandrels. The south porch is dated 1795. The chancel was rebuilt in 1806 and remodelled in 1865. There are several good monuments, but none earlier than the late 18th century, the period of the pulpit and west gallery.

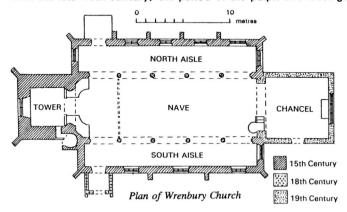

Plan of Wrenbury Church

Wrenbury Church

Tower at Wrenbury

Tower at Wybunbury

WYBUNBURY   *St Chad*   SJ 700499

James Brooks rebuilt the church in 1892-3 but it was demolished c1970 except for the lofty 15th century five-stage west tower with statues, partly recarved, of two bishops, the Annunciation, and the Trinity on the west side. The 15th century font, a brass with figures of Rafe Delves, d1513 and his wife, and the tomb with fine recumbent effigies of Thomas Smith, d1614, and his wife have been removed.

LIST OF LATER CHURCHES IN CHESHIRE

ALDERLEY EDGE - St Philip - 1851-2 by J.S.Crowther.
ALDFORD - St John Baptist - rebuilt 1866 by John Douglas.
ALSAGER - Christchurch - 1789-90 by Thomas Stringer.
ALSAGER - St Mary Magdalene - 1894-8 by Austin & Paley.
ALTRINCHAM - St Alban - 1900 by Austin & Paley.
ALTRINCHAM - St George - 1799, extended 1858 and 1869, rebuilt 1886.
ALTRINCHAM - St John Evengelist - 1865-6 by J.Medland Taylor.
ALVANLEY - St John Evangelist - 1861 architect unknown.
ANTROBUS - St Mark - 1847-8 by Scott.
APPLETON THORN - St Cross - 1887 by Edmund Kirby.
ASHLEY - St Elizabeth - 1870s by Wilbraham Egerton.
ASHTON - St John Evangelist - 1849 by Shellard.
BARNSTON - Christchurch - 1870-1 by G.E.Street.
BARNTON - Christchurch - 1842 and 1900.
BEBINGTON - Christchurch - 1857-9 by Walter Scott.
BICKERTON - Holy Trinity - 1839 by Edmund Sharpe.
BICKLEY - St Wenefrede - 1892 by Douglas & Fordham.
BIRKENHEAD - Holy Trinity - 1837-40 by Cunninghame & Holme.
BIRKENHEAD - St Anne - 1840s by William Cole.
BIRKENHEAD - St James - 1845 by C.E.Lang.
BIRKENHEAD - St John Evangelist - 1845-7 by Charles Reed.
BIRKENHEAD - St Mary - 1819-21 by Thomas Rickman, and 1882-3.
BIRKENHEAD - St Peter - 1866-8 by David Walker.
BOLLINGTON - Holy Trinity - 1854 by Salvin.
BOLLINGTON - St John Baptist - 1832-4 by Hayley & Brown.
BOLLINGTON CROSS - St Oswald - 1908 by F.P. Oakley.
BOUGHTON - St Paul - 1876 and 1902 by Douglas.
BREDBURY - St Mark - 1847-8 by Shellard.
BROADBOTTOM - St Mary Magdalene - 1888-90 by W.H.Lowder.
BUGLAWTON - St John Evangelist - 1840 by R.B.Rampling.
BYLEY - St John Evangelist - 1846-7 by Henry Massey or J.Matthews.
CALDY - Resurrection & All Saints - 1868 by G.E.Street, and 1906-7.
CAPENHURST - Holy Trinity - 1856-9 by James Harrison.
CHEADLE - All Hallows - 1969 by Paterson & Macauley.
CHEADLE HULME - All Saints - 1862-3 and 1873 by Medland Taylor.
CHELFORD - St John Evangelist - 1774-6 and 1840.
CHESTER - Christchurch - rebuilt 1876-1900 by Douglas.
CHESTER - St Mary-Without-The-Walls - 1885-6 by F.B.Wade.
CHESTER - St Thomas of Canterbury - 1869-72 by Sir G.G.Scott.
CHILDER THORNTON (Hooton) - St Paul - 1858-62 by James K.Colling.
CLAUGHTON - Christchurch - 1844-9 by William Jearrad.
CLAUGHTON - St Mark - 1890-1 by Harvey, Pennington & Bridgen.
CODDINGTON - St Mary - 13th century, entirely rebuilt in 1833 by J.Atkinson.
COMPSTALL - St Paul - 1839-40, chancel 1866 by James Hunt.
CONGLETON - Holy Trinity - 1844-5 by C. & J. Trubshaw.
CONGLETON - St Stephen - 1858-60 by Joseph Clarke.
COTEBROOK - St John - 1874-5 by Street.
CREWE - All Saints - 1964-5 by Robert Maguire and Keith Murray.
CREWE - Christchurch - 1843 probably by Cunningham.
CREWE - St Barnabas - 1885 by Paley & Austin.
CREWE - St John Baptist - 1894-1901 by Hicks & Charlewood.
CREWE - St Michael - 1882-6 and 1907-10 by James Brooks.

CREWE - St Paul - 1868-9 by Stansby.
CREWE - St Peter - 1914-23 by J.Brooke and C.E.Elcock.
CREWE GREEN - St Michael - 1857-8 by Sir George Gilbert Scott.
CROWTON - Christchurch - 1871 by Pearson.
DELAMERE - St Peter - rebuilt 1816-17 by J. Gunnery, altered 1878.
DUDDON - St Peter - 1835 by William Railton.
DUKINFIELD - St John - 1838-40 by E.Sharpe.
DUKINFIELD - St Luke - 1889 by Eaton & Sons.
DUKINFIELD - St Mark - 1848-9 by Joseph Clarke.
DUNHAM MASSEY - St Margaret - 1853-5 by Hayley and 1923 by Tapper.
DUNHAM MASSEY - St Mark - 1864 by George & John Shaw.
DUNHAM-ON-THE-HILL - St Luke - 1860-1 by James Harrison.
EATON - Christchurch - 1856-8 by Raffles Brown.
EATON - St Thomas - 1896 architect unknown.
EGREMONT - St John - 1832-3 by H.Edwards.
ELLESMERE PORT - Christchurch - 1869-71 by Penson & Richie.
ELWORTH - St Peter - 1845-6 by John Matthews.
FRANKBY - St John Divine - 1861-2 by W. & J.Hay.
GATLEY GREEN - St James - 1880-1 by Medland Taylor.
GEE CROSS (Hyde) - Holy Trinity - 1873-4 by M. & H.Taylor.
GODLEY - St John Baptist - 1849-50 by E.H.Shellard.
GREAT SAUGHALL - All Saints - 1895-1901 by Medland Taylor.
GREAT SUTTON - St John Evangelist - 1879-80 by David Walker.
HALE - St Peter - 1890-2 by Tate & Popplewell.
HALEBARNS - All Saints - 1966-7 by Brian Bonskill.
HALTON - St Mary - rebuilt 1851-2 by Sir George Gilbert Scott.
HANDFORTH - St Chad - 1897-8 by John Brooke.
HARTFORD - St John Baptist - 1874-5 by John Douglas.
HASLINGTON - St Matthew - 1810 and 1909 by Reginald Longden.
HAZEL GROVE - St Thomas - 1833-4 by Hayley & Brown.
HELSBY - St Paul - 1868-70 by Douglas, and 1909.
HENBURY - St Thomas - 1844-5 by Richard Lane.
HIGHER WALTON - St John Evangelist - 1885 by Paley & Austin.
HIGH LANE - St Thomas - 1852, and 1866 by Medland Taylor.
HIGH LEGH - St John - 1893 by Kirby.
HOLLINGWORTH - St Mary - 1863-4 by Clegg & Knowles.
HOOLE - All Saints - 1867 by Dawkes.
HOYLAKE - Holy Trinity - 1833 by Sir James Picton.
HOYLAKE - St Hildeburgh - 1897-9 by Edmund Kirby.
HOYLAKE (Meols) - St John Baptist - 1911-13 by Edmund Kirby.
HULME WALFIELD - St Michael - 1855-6 by Sir George Gilbert Scott.
HURDSFIELD - Holy Trinity - 1837-40 by William Hayley
HYDE - St George - 1831-2 by T. & C.Atkinson.
HYDE - St Mary - 1838-9 by Hayley & Brown.
HYDE - St Stephen - 1889-91 by J.Eaton.
HYDE - St Thomas - 1867-8 by Medland and Henry Taylor.
KELSALL - St Philip - 1860 by T.Bower.
KINGSLEY - St John Evangelist - 1849-50 by Sir George Gilbert Scott.
KNUTSFORD - St Cross - 1888-1 by Paley and Austin.
LISCARD - St Mary - 1876-7 by E.W.Nobbs.
LITTLE LEIGH - St Michael - 1878-9 by Kirby.
LOSTOCK GRALAM - St John Evangelist - 1844-5 (and probably 1870s).

MACCLESFIELD - Christchurch - 1775-6 for patron Charles Roe.
MACCLESFIELD - St George - 1822-3 (originally Congregationist).
MACCLESFIELD - St Paul - 1843-4 by W. Hayley.
MACCLESFIELD - St Peter - 1849 by C. & J.Trubshaw.
MARPLE - All Saints - 1808-12 Tower only on site of 16th century timber chapel.
MARPLE - New All Saints (beside above) 1878-80 by Medland and Henry Taylor.
MARPLE - St Martin - 1869-70 by J.D.Sedding.
MARTHALL - All Saints - 1839, enlarged in 1887.
MILLBROOK - St James - 1861-3 by G. & J.Shaw.
MINSHULL VERNON - St Peter - 1840s by John Matthews.
MOULTON - St Stephen - 1876-7 by Douglas.
MOW COP - St Luke - 1875 architect unknown.
NEW BRIGHTON - All Saints - 1927-39 by Sir Giles Gilbert Scott.
NEW BRIGHTON - Emmanuel - 1899-1909 by C.E.Deacon.
NEW BRIGHTON - St James - 1854-6 by Sir George Gilbert Scott.
NEW FERRY - St Mark - 1865-6 by Edward Haycock the younger.
NORLEY - St John Evangelist - 1878-9 by Pearson.
NORTH RODE - St Michael - 1845 by C. & J.Trubshaw.
NORTHWICH - Holy Trinity - 1842 architect unknown.
OUGHTRINGTON - St Peter - 1871-2 by Slater & Carpenter.
OVER TABLEY - St Paul - 1855-6 by Salvin.
OXTON - All Saints - 1879 architect unknown.
OXTON - St Saviour - 1889-92 by C.W.Harvey.
PARKGATE - St Thomas - 1843 architect unknown.
PARTINGTON - St Mary - 1884 by G.Truefitt.
PORT SUNLIGHT - Christchurch - 1902-4 by William & Segar Owen.
POULTON - St Luke - 1899 by Harry May (contains Norman font).
POYNTON - St George - 1858-9 by Crowther. Steeple 1884-5.
PRENTON - St Alban - 1961 by Gerald Beech.
PRENTON - St Stephen - 1897-1909 by Deacon & Horsburgh.
PULFORD - St Mary - rebuilt 1881-4 by Douglas. Had 15th century tower.
RAINOW - Holy Trinity - 1845-6 by Samuel Howard.
RINGWAY - St Mary - 1894-5 by Preston & Vaughan.
ROCK FERRY - St Barnabas - 1903 by Grayson & Ould.
ROCK FERRY - St Peter - 1841-2 by Hurst & Moffatt.
RODE - All Saints - 1864 by Sir George Gilbert Scott.
ROMILEY - St Chad - 1864-6 by Medland Taylor.
RUNCORN - Holy Trinity - 1838 by Joseph Hartley.
RUNCORN - St Michael - 1884-92 by T.D.Barry.
SALE - St Anne - 1854 by Hayley, and 1860s and 1887.
SALE - St Paul - 1883-4 by H.R.Price. Tower 1911 by Bird & Oldham.
SALTNEY - St Mark - 1892-3 by Lockwood.
SANDBACH HEATH - St John - 1861 by Sir George Gilbert Scott.
SANDIWAY - St John Evangelist - 1902-3 by John Douglas.
SMALLWOOD - St John Baptist - 1845 by C. & J.Trubshaw.
STALYBRIDGE - St George - 1838-40 by Sharpe.
STALYBRIDGE - St Paul - 1839 probably by Tattersall.
STOCKPORT - St Alban - 1899 by Preston & Vaughan.
STOCKPORT - St Augustine - 1893 by Preston & Vaughan.
STOCKPORT - St George - 1896-7 by Austin and Paley.
STOCKPORT - St Paul - 1849-51 by Bowman & Crowther.
STOCKPORT - St Saviour - begun 1915 by R.B.Preston

STOCKPORT - St Thomas - 1822-5 by George Basevi.
STOCKTON HEATH - St Thomas - 1868 by E.G.Paley.
STRETTON - St Matthew - 1826, entirely rebuilt in 1870 by Scott.
SUTTON LANE ENDS - St James - 1840 by Hayley.
THELWALL - All Saints - 1843 by J.Mountford Allen.
THORNTON HOUGH - All Saints - 1867 by Kirk & Sons.
THREAPWOOD - St John - 1815 architect unknown.
THURSTASTON - St Bartholomew - rebuilt 1885 by John Loughborough.
TILSTONE FEARNALL - St Jude - c1836 architect unknown.
TIMPERLEY - Christchurch - 1849 by Bayley, extended 1864 by John Lowe.
TINTWISTLE - Christchurch - 1837 architect unknown.
TOFT - St John Evangelist - 1854-5 by W & G.Habershon.
TRANMERE - St Catherine - 1831 enlarged 1875-6 by J.Francis Doyle.
TRANMERE - St Luke - 1881 by C.E.Grayson.
TRANMERE - St Paul - 1854-5 by W.& J.Hay.
TUPTON - St Mary - 1868 by John Cunningham.
UPTON - Holy Ascension - 1852-4 by James Harrison.
WALLASEY (Moreton) - Christchurch - 1862-3 by Cunningham & Audsley.
WALLASEY (Egremont) - St Columba - 1902-23 by C.E.Dobson.
WALLASEY - St Nicholas - 1910-11 by J.Francis Doyle.
WALLASEY (Seacombe) - St Paul - 1846-7 by Hay bros, enlarged 1859 & 1891.
WARBURTON - New St Werburgh - 1883-5 by Douglas.
WEST KIRBY - St Andrew - 1889-91 by Douglas & Fordham. Completed in 1907-9.
WESTON - All Saints - c1840 with a chancel of 1893.
WESTON - St John Evangelist - 1895-8 by Douglas & Fordham.
WETTENHALL - St David - 1870 by J.Redford & J.A.Davenport.
WHARTON - Christchurch - 1840s, transepts possibly older.
WHEELOCK - Christchurch - 1836-7 and chancel 1903 by Alfred Price.
WILDBOARCLOUGH - St Saviour - 1908-9 architect unknown.
WILLASTON - Christchurch - 1854 by Fulljames & Walker.
WILMSLOW (Lindow) - St John Evangelist - 1873-4 by J.W.Beaumont.
WINSFORD - Christchurch - 1844, entirely rebuilt 1882 by Richard Beckett.
WINSFORD - St John Evangelist - 1860-3 by John Douglas.
WISTASTON - St Mary - 1827-8 by George Latham.
WOODFORD - Christchurch - 1841 architect unknown.
WOODHEAD - St James - late 18th or early 19th century dale chapel.
WORLESTON - St Oswald - 1872 by C.Lynam.

PRIVATE DETACHED CHAPELS

CAPESTHORNE - Holy Trinity, a brick building with stone dressings and an apse built for John Ward in 1722.

CHOLMONDLEY - St Nicholas, a brick building of 1716 designed by Vanburgh to which transepts were added in 1829. Galleries inserted 1840. Original timber framed 13th century building damaged during attacks on house during Civil War.

WOODHEY - Hipped-roofed brick building of four bays with a triple arched west portico, and round arched windows, plus circular window over SW doorway. Built in 1700 for Lady Wilbraham.

A GLOSSARY OF ARCHITECTURAL TERMS

Apse	- Semi-circular or polygonal east end of a church containing an altar.
Ashlar	- Masonry of blocks with even faces and square edges.
Ballflower	- Globular flower of three petals enclosing ball. Current c1310-40.
Baroque	- A whimsical and odd form of the Classical architectural style.
Beakhead	- Decorative motif of bird or beast heads, often biting a roll moulding.
Broaches	- Sloping half pyramids adapting an octagonal spire to a square tower.
Ceilure	- A small section of ceiling, sometimes highly decorated.
Chancel	- The eastern part of a church used by the clergy.
Chevron Ornament	- A Norman ornament with continuous Vs forming a zig-zag.
Clerestory	- An upper storey pierced by windows lighting the floor below.
Coffering	- Sunk square or polygonal panels on a ceiling.
Collar Beam	- A tie-beam used higher up near the apex of the roof.
Crossing Tower	- A tower built on four arches in the middle of a cruciform church.
Cruciform Church	- A cross-shaped church with transepts forming the arms of the cross.
Cusp	- A projecting point between the foils of a foiled Gothic arch.
Dado	- The decorative covering of the lower part of a wall or screen.
Dog Tooth	- Four centered stars placed diagonally and raised pyramidally.
Easter Sepulchre	- A recess in a chancel which received an effigy of Christ at Easter.
Elizabethan	- Of the time of Queen Elizabeth I (1558-1603).
Fan Vault	- Vault with fan-like patterns. In fashion from c1440 to 1530.
Foil	- A lobe formed by the cusping of a circle or arch.
Four Centred Arch	- A low, flattish arch with each curve drawn from two compass points.
Head Stops	- Heads of humans or beasts forming the ends of a hoodmould.
Hoodmould	- A projecting moulding above a lintel or arch to throw off water.
Impost	- A wall bracket, often moulded, to support the end of an arch.
Jacobean	- Of the time of King James I (1603-25).
Jamb	- The side of a doorway, window, or other opening.
King Post	- An upright timber connecting a tie-beam with a collar-beam.
Lancet	- A long and comparatively narrow window with a pointed head.
Lierne Vault	- A vault with a complex system of major and minor ribs and bosses.
Light	- A compartment of a window.
Lintel	- A horizontal stone or beam spanning an opening.
Low-side window	- A window with a low sill allowing those outside a chancel to see inside.
Miserichord	- Bracket underneath hinged choir stall seat to support standing person.
Mullion	- A vertical member dividing the lights of a window.
Nave	- The part of a church in which the congregation sits or stands.
Norman	- A division of English Romanesque architecture from 1066 to 1200.
Ogival Arch	- Arch of oriental origin with both convex and concave curves.
Pilaster	- Flat buttress or pier attached to a wall.
Piscina	- A stone basin used for rinsing out holy vessels after a mass.
Plinth	- The projecting base of a wall.
Queen Posts	- Two vertical timbers connecting a tie-beam and a collar-beam.
Quoins	- Dressed stones at the corners of a building.
Respond	- A half pier or column bonded into a wall and carrying an arch.
Reticulation	- Tracery with a net-like appearence. Current c1330-70.
Rococo	- The late phase of the Baroque style, current in mid 18th century.
Rood Screen	- A screen with a crucifix mounted on it between a nave and chancel.
Sedilia	- Seats for clergy (usually three) in the south wall of a chancel.
Spandrel	- The surface between two arches.
Tester	- A sounding board above a 17th or 18th century pulpit.
Tie-Beam	- A beam connecting the slopes of a roof at or near its foot.
Tracery	- Intersecting ribwork in the upper part of a later Gothic window.
Transom	- A horizontal member dividing the lights of a window.
Triptych	- Three surfaces, usually sculpted or painted, joined by hinges.
Tuscan	- An order of Classical architecture.
Tympanum	- The space between the lintel of a doorway and the arch above it.
Venetian Window	- Window with a square headed light on either side of an arched light.